SOVEREIGN WEALTH FUNDS

Hh | Harriman House

Harriman House is one of the UK's leading independent publishers of financial and business books. Our catalogue covers personal finance, stock market investing and trading, current affairs, business and economics. For more details go to:

www.harriman-house.com

Sovereign Wealth Funds

A complete guide to state-owned investment funds

by Alberto Quadrio Curzio and Valeria Miceli

Hh

HARRIMAN HOUSE LTD

3A Penns Road
Petersfield
Hampshire
GU32 2EW
GREAT BRITAIN

Tel: +44 (0)1730 233870
Fax: +44 (0)1730 233880
Email: enquiries@harriman-house.com
Website: www.harriman-house.com

First published in Great Britain in 2010
Originally published as «I fondi sovrani» in Italy in 2009

Copyright © Harriman House Ltd

The right of Alberto Quadrio Curzio and Valeria Miceli to be identified as the authors
has been asserted in accordance with the Copyright, Design and Patents Act 1988.

ISBN: 978-1-906659-96-7

British Library Cataloguing in Publication Data
A CIP catalogue record for this book can be obtained from the British Library.

Printed and bound in the UK by CPI Antony Rowe, Chippenham

Contents

List of Figures and Tables

About the Authors

Alberto Quadrio Curzio is Full Professor of Political Economy, Dean of the Political Science Faculty and Director of the Research Centre in Economic Analysis at the Catholic University in Milan. He is Vice President of the National Academy of Lincei and Director of *Economia Politica* (Journal of Analytical and Institutional Economics). He is a former President of the Italian Economic Association.

Valeria Miceli is a lecturer at the Faculty of Political Science and a member of the Scientific Committee of the Research Centre in Economic Analysis at the Catholic University in Milan. She received her PhD from the same university.

Introduction

What This Book Covers

This book is a thorough guide to sovereign wealth funds, an area of finance worth trillions of dollars, involving many of the world's governments, and affecting a wide array of sectors, but which – and not accidentally – often remains profoundly obscure.

Sovereign wealth funds (from here on SWFs) are state-owned investment vehicles that manage portfolios of financial activities. They are typically denominated in foreign currency deriving either from the sale of petroleum and other raw materials (commodity SWFs) or from other surpluses of the balance of payments (non-commodity SWFs).

From this common denominator, differences between funds can be outlined according to purpose, legal structure, strategy and source(s) of financing. This makes it possible to classify various types of SWFs: stabilisation funds, savings funds, reserve funds, development funds, and pension reserve funds without explicit pension liabilities.

The main players in this scenario amongst emerging countries are the Persian Gulf states, China, Singapore, Russia and Libya, and, amongst developed nations, Norway.

In 2009 there were 53 SWFs in the world, with total assets of between US$3,200 billion and US$3,800 billion. These are highly respectable numbers, especially if one considers that they are concentrated in the hands of just a few large operators. The ten largest SWFs hold 74% of total assets held by all SWFs. Since most of the assets managed by SWFs (almost 80% of the total) belong to emerging countries, while only 18% (in terms of asset size) belong to full democracies (according to *The Economist* Intelligence Unit's index of democracy), it is understandable how worrying their investments have been to recipient countries, especially considering how opaque and inscrutable many can be. Indeed, SWFs are equally a political as well as a financial concern. Since they are an expression of a new state capitalism, they are suspected, rightly or wrongly, of representing interests that go beyond their avowed goal of profit maximisation. As yet, though, no empirical evidence has been produced to substantiate such anxieties.

First ignored, then viewed as "barbarians at the gate"[1], and finally considered as lenders of last resort for the shaky financial sector, the image of SWFs has constantly changed, and they have had to quickly adapt to changing circumstances.

Since the beginning of the 21st century, SWFs have grown in number and size. With the price of petroleum rising constantly up until mid-2008, Asian countries' exports and surpluses also growing steadily, and the persistence of worldwide financial imbalances between countries that consume too much and save too little (the United States) and other countries that consume too little and save too much (China), it is not surprising that SWFs transformed into overactive financial giants in global markets, especially in the years 2007 and 2008. Their increasing role in financial markets – along with their opaque approach, the entry into the game of economic and political heavyweights such as China and Russia, and apprehensions about the shift of financial power which SWFs therefore symbolise – all contributed to their growing importance and visibility. They captured the concerned attention of institutional players (national and supranational), and of public opinion in Western democracies as well as in their own countries.

During 2007-2008, called upon by Western governments and institutions, they initially helped both their public image and the struggling economies of Western nations by contributing to recapitalise their crisis-stricken banks and by investing in important but troubled financial companies. Then from September 2008 – with losses accumulated mainly from these financial shareholdings, the fall in the price of oil, the shrinking of Asian exporters' current account surpluses and the need to provide support to domestic economies – SWFs underwent a phase of retrenchment. It was only in the second half of 2009, having adjusted targets and strategies to the changed financial scenario, that they re-entered the stage, proving to be major players in international financial markets.

The purpose of this book is to present a comprehensive survey of these increasingly important institutions. The Italian edition of the book was published in 2009 by il Mulino with the title «I fondi sovrani». The present English edition is broader and more detailed than the Italian one, not only because so much has changed in the intervening year, but also because we have had the opportunity to take into account even more of the growing academic literature on the subject.

Structure of the Book

After a brief historical digression bringing us up to the present (Chapter 1), this book focuses firstly on the fundamental issue of defining SWFs (Chapter 2). After this, we identify the actors involved, before classifying them and studying their main characteristics. In Chapter 3 we have chosen a few of the most representative SWFs based on the size of their assets, and examine in detail their history, purposes, organisation, portfolios and transparency.

The importance of SWFs on international financial markets leads us in Chapter 4 to study their investment strategies, with the help of various academic studies, so as to be able to quantify their impact on financial markets. At least for now, empirical evidence seems to suggest that stabilising factors outweigh the negative ones, even if this evidence is not univocal and further research is required.

In Chapter 5 we deal with the feared intertwining of economics and politics in SWFs and the possible geopolitical consequences of their rise. There is widespread belief that transparency and good governance are the keys to alleviating fear and keeping markets open. But measuring the transparency of each SWF presents us with the worrying fact that the largest SWFs are on average the least transparent, and the least transparent SWFs are typically based in non-democratic countries. Of course, when dealing with transparency and good governance, two aspects cannot be forgotten, and in this chapter will not be. Firstly transparency and good governance must be assessed not only from Western countries' point of view, but also from the perspective of the citizens of the countries owning the SWFs, the final owners of their wealth. Secondly, in the plea for transparency, all the actors involved in financial markets must be treated according to the same principles.

Various governments – including those of the United States, Germany and France – have discussed and in some cases taken action to limit foreign direct investment by SWFs. International institutions, however, have tried to formulate a multilateral framework for the issue. The approach of individual countries, and the European Commission, will be examined in Chapter 6, and that of the International Monetary Fund (IMF) and the Organisation for Economic Co-operation and Development (OECD) in Chapter 7.

Who This Book is For

This book adopts a careful empirical approach to an area hitherto mired in obscurity and suspicion, and attempts to clarify and synthesise all that can be known about a very complex matter. It should therefore prove of use to a wide audience. This will range from economic and financial operators, to academic scholars and policymakers.

As will become clear in the course of this book, no cartoon villain or hero will in fact materialise. SWFs are neither enemies nor saviours. They are simply investors with a marked and lasting influence on financial markets. Being familiar with them is crucial to understanding their behaviour, as well as rendering them responsible actors in more efficiently-regulated markets and a broader integrated world economy.

* * *

This new edition of the book is the joint work of the two authors, who have joint responsibility for the contents. Valeria Miceli has entirely written Chapters 3, 4 (as in the Italian edition) and this version of Chapter 5. These chapters have been significantly expanded in this English edition.

The authors express their thanks to the Catholic University of Milan, which in part sponsored this research within the Project D.3.2. entitled «Geosviluppo, innovazione e competitività» ('Geo-development, innovation and competitiveness'), to Carolyn Kadas for having translated the book from Italian and for revising the broader English edition, and to Chris Parker for his comments.

This study was undertaken by the authors at the Centro di Ricerche in Analisi Economica ed Economia Internazionale (Centre for Research in Economic Analysis and International Economic Development), also known as CRANEC, at the Catholic University of Milan.

Milan
15 February 2010

1.

How and When Sovereign Wealth Funds Came About

The history of sovereign wealth funds can be divided into four phases, beginning in 1953. In that year, the first authority that foreshadowed a SWF was founded: the Kuwait Investment Authority (KIA). From then on, SWFs, new entities in finance and the world economy, grew and spread throughout various countries. SWFs were to assume three basic features: they originated from foreign currency surpluses; they were owned and managed by sovereign states or their emanations; and they were financially earmarked mainly for extra-national purposes.

According to analysis by Griffith and Ocampo[2], the accumulation of foreign-exchange assets and the subsequent decision to establish a SWF is typically based on four types of motives:

1. 'wealth substitution' or transforming natural resources into financial assets

2. 'resilient surplus', in case of long-lasting current account surpluses that cannot be corrected in the short-run by exchange-rate appreciation

3. 'counter-cyclicality', to absorb temporary current account surpluses and/or booming commodity prices

4. 'self-insurance', associated with reducing the risks of pro-cyclical capital flows.

The last two strategies, even if rational from the point of view of the individual country, help fuel global imbalances and the consequent instability of the world economy. As we will see, in each of the phases in the development of SWFs, the above motives have had different relative importance. This has given rise to different types of SWFs in terms of origin, nature and purpose, and consequently in their investment strategies.

The initial phase that started in 1953 intensified in the 1970s, with the start-up of several SWFs in countries with surpluses from oil exports (which grew with the increase in the price of crude oil, and continued until the first half of the 1990s). In this period, the motives for creating most of the funds were wealth substitution and counter-cyclicality.

The second phase began in the late 1990s and ended in 2004. In addition to the oil SWFs, there were growing numbers of SWFs emerging from Asian countries, which benefited from enormous trade-balance surpluses from exports of manufactured goods. By accumulating and managing currency reserves, these SWFs pursued a strategy of covering the risks from the kinds of financial and currency crises which had characterised their recent past (self-insurance).

The third phase covered the recent years from 2005 to 2008, when the term 'sovereign wealth funds' was first coined and SWFs came to the attention of the broader public (and not just financial operators). In this phase we also saw a change in the attitude of countries receiving SWF investment: from caution if not hostility towards SWFs, to appreciation as lenders of last resort able to help them resist banking and financial turmoil.

The financial crisis beginning in 2007 opened a fourth phase that was still underway in 2010. In this phase, SWFs have had to come to terms with significant losses, and financial markets in difficulty everywhere. This has caused their investment activity to substantially contract. Only since the second half of 2009 have they really returned to the fray, with targets and strategies adjusted to the changed financial scene. They have proven, so far, to now be major players in international financial markets, willing to behave responsibly and cooperatively.

From 1953 to the Mid-1990s: Unknown Actors

This first phase has two milestones. The initial one came in 1953 with the establishment of the Kuwait Investment Board, which then became the Kuwait Investment Authority (KIA). This was actually not a real SWF, but an authority, according to the criteria listed in Chapter 2. Nevertheless, KIA was in substance a SWF, because its specific purpose was to invest surpluses derived from oil revenues so as to reduce Kuwait's dependence on exhaustible fossil reserves, thus lessening the effects of price oscillation. Thus oil revenues were converted into financial investments; mostly fixed-interest, low-risk securities.

The second SWF, established with a specific legal status, was created by the British colonial administration of the Gilbert Islands in 1956, to capitalise on the revenues from phosphate by investing them in diversified shareholdings. The Revenue Equalization Reserve Fund was and is certainly not comparable in size to those generated by oil revenues or other revenues mentioned later. But compared to the size of the economy of its host (now the Republic of Kiribati), the stock of assets accumulated by this SWF is in the present-day three times greater than their GDP.

In the 1970s the rise in the price of oil from under US$5 a barrel to more than US$35 in 1980, the year after the Khomeini revolution, made it possible for exporting countries to rapidly accumulate enormous financial wealth. These revenues were partly spent domestically, with the resulting push of domestic inflation. Consequently oil revenues were increasingly allocated to foreign direct investment. We can see in this accumulation of foreign assets and the subsequent decision to establish SWFs with them, the prevalence of wealth substitution and counter-cyclical motives. The purpose indeed was to create diversified sources of income other than oil, in order to counterbalance the depletion of this raw material and its price fluctuation, but also to protect domestic wellbeing. An additional motive might have been political, too, as governments in emerging oil-exporting countries often need to maintain control of wealth in order to strengthen their internal political power as well as gain support from developed countries interested in receiving petro-dollar investment.

Various countries, in particular the members of the Gulf Cooperation Council (GCC), launched new SWFs: the United Arab Emirates (UAE) established the Abu Dhabi Investment Authority in 1976, and in the same year Kuwait founded another fund, the Future Generations Fund, which was managed by KIA.

Even in developed countries, the increase in oil prices and prices of raw materials in the early 1970s brought about the launch of two oil-based SWFs in 1976: the Alaska Permanent Fund Corporation in the United States, and Alberta's Heritage Fund in Canada.

In this phase, another type of SWF was also established: the non-commodity SWF. In 1974 the Singapore government founded Temasek Holdings, while in 1981 the Government of Singapore Investment Corporation (GIC) was also set up. Both fitted into Singapore's growth strategy, as a city-state with too small a domestic market to generate sufficient consumption and investment demand to use its currency and fiscal surpluses. Of a similar nature, Malaysia's Khazanah Nasional Berhad was set up several years later in 1993.

The 1980s and 1990s featured two large-scale international dynamics which affected SWFs: a fall in the price of oil in the 1980s and the wave of growing globalisation in the 1990s.

The oil price fell below US$20 a barrel in the mid-1980s, staying below this level until the end of the 1990s except for a price upsurge during the Iraqi invasion of Kuwait. These downward price fluctuations reinforced the belief of governments running SWFs that their income should not depend solely on oil and natural gas. This meant reinforcing the counter-cyclical component at the base of the decision to establish SWFs. Thus other SWFs were launched, including the State General Reserve Fund of Oman in 1980, and, in 1981, the Libyan Arab Foreign Investment Company, fuelled by proceeds from natural gas fields discovered in the 1970s and 1980s. In 1983, the Brunei Investment Agency was established, and in 1984 so too was the Abu Dhabi International Petroleum Investment Company.

The advent of globalisation contributed significantly to the growth of SWFs, facilitating the international movement of capital and direct investment abroad. The year 1990 was the second great milestone in the initial phase of SWF history, with the establishment of the Norwegian Government Pension Fund, currently the second-largest SWF in the world. This initiative must be seen as an answer to the needs of wealth substitution and counter-cyclicality, as well as an attempt to avoid 'Dutch disease'. (Dutch disease being the fate which befell a Holland briefly rich with North Sea natural gas in the 1960s. The currency of the commodity-rich nation rose too far, distorting the economy.) Indeed, in the case of an advanced country like Norway, it makes economic sense to prefer long-term savings to domestic spending on internal investment.

During this first period, spanning more than 40 years, 16 SWFs (refer to the classification provided in Chapter 2) were established. Their investment strategies remained conservative and prudent with portfolios largely composed of low-yield, mainly US government securities. In this period they sought and maintained a very low profile. As a consequence they were almost unknown even to the financial community.

From the Late '90s to 2004: Emerging From Anonymity

Emerging countries' impressive accumulation of foreign exchange reserves was a characteristic phenomenon of the first decade of the 2000s. Following the currency crisis that hit emerging economies in the 1990s (particularly in the latter half of the decade), many countries, and especially those hardest hit, proceeded to systematically accumulate reserves well in excess of short-term external liabilities (the level suggested by the so-called Guidotti-Greenspan rule).

Figure 1 – Total foreign exchange holdings in US$ billion (1995 to third quarter 2009)

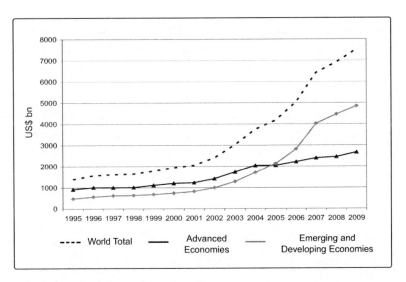

Source: Our elaboration on IMF, Currency Composition of Official Foreign Exchange Reserves (COFER) Database, accessed February 2010.

Self-insurance is one of the most commonly accepted explanations of why developing countries decide to hold an excessive level of foreign reserves with all the costs this choice implies[3]. Another possible explanation is mercantilism (fostering export competitiveness). For some countries the rationale of hoarding reserves stems from an aggregation of several motives: in the aftermath of the East Asian crisis self-insurance dominated, while after 2000 other motives must also be taken into account[4].

Just after the various financial crises of the late '90s, emerging countries, facing growing financial instability in a more interconnected world, rationally decided to self-insure themselves to avoid having to resort to the IMF with its principle of conditionality, thus minimising the risks and associated costs of future crises. Excess reserves may therefore be correlated with the volatility of capital flows and eventually to the level of a country's financial openness. Obstfeld et al[5] have conducted an empirical study that clearly shows a statistical and economically significant correlation of reserve levels with financial openness and financial development, especially in the years after the Asian crises. Indeed, countries that gradually liberalised capital markets have been less exposed to financial crises. If hoarding reserves is a rational answer from an individual country's point of view, however, from the collective point of view this strategy appears dangerous, since it contributes to feeding global imbalances, with some countries accumulating large debts and others accumulating excessive currency-exchange surpluses.

Since this huge level of reserves generates two types of costs both in terms of lower yields and the sterilisation necessary to avoid inflation, the debate in economic literature is open as to why countries choose to self-insure themselves instead of closing capital markets. The answer according to Rodrik[6] is that closing to financial liberalisation is difficult due to interest-group pressure and the practical difficulty nowadays of controlling and preventing massive capital outflows.

In the face of the significant costs entailed in maintaining huge reserves, several emerging countries decided to allocate part of their currency reserves to new investment vehicles able to prefer yields over liquidity. Thus the Chinese SAFE Investment Company was established in 1997 and the Hong Kong Monetary Authority Investment Portfolio in 1998. Following the same logic, the Korea Investment Corporation was created in 2005.

While some Asian countries which accumulated huge currency reserves only recently set up SWFs with modest asset levels compared to the size of their respective reserves, the Middle Eastern countries and other oil- and gas-exporting countries chose the opposite strategy. They chose to invest their wealth mainly in other investment vehicles including sovereign funds, to the detriment of their currency reserves.

At the same time, growing demand in emerging economies, especially Asian ones, pushed up oil prices from less than US$20 a barrel at the end of the 1990s to almost US$40 in 2004. Oil-exporting countries, including those of the GCC, benefited from this significant increase in the price of oil and gas, pouring revenues into funding their SWFs. This time, these countries were determined to avoid the waste and inefficiency that characterised what happened to the oil windfalls of the '70s and decided to transfer part of this windfall to SWFs. At the turn of the century the number of SWFs grew substantially; between 1998 and 2004 15 SWFs were established. Most of them were commodity based. The Iranian Oil Stabilization Fund and Azerbaijan's State Oil Fund were both set up in 1999, the Algerian Revenue Regulation Fund and Kazakhstan's National Fund in 2000, Abu Dhabi's Mubadala in 2002 and Istithmar World (owned by Dubai World) in 2003. In 2004 Nigeria's Excess Crude Account and Russia's Stabilization Fund of the Russian Federation (oil-based) were set up.

In 2003 the New Zealand Superannuation Fund was created. In this case the rationale was different and was related to the need to meet this government's future liabilities for the payment of pensions in an ageing society. The same rationale was at the base of the establishment, in the following phase in 2006, of the Australian Government Future Fund.

At the end of this period the total assets held by SWFs were estimated at US$895 billion, according to Rozanov[7].

From 2005 to Mid-2008: Emerging Overactive Giants

In this period SWFs entered the limelight of world news, and caught the interested and concerned attention of institutional players (national and supranational) and public opinion in Western democracies. There was a growing realisation of the influence these players could have on global markets as major investors. Overall reactions were quite troubled; one critic viewed them as "barbarians at the gate"[8], ready to take control of Western interests.

In 2005 the expression *sovereign wealth funds* was coined by Andrew Rozanov[9] of State Street Global Advisors. This designated investment entities, different from public pension funds and currency reserves, that have among their objectives coverage from excess volatility of energy raw-material revenues, accumulation of wealth for future generations, and economic and social development. Rozanov recognised that many of these funds were not new, but their increasing numbers throughout the world and the rapid growth of their assets justified specific attention. His article marked the starting point of a growing interest on the part of operators and scholars, which led to a proliferation of research on the topic. Whereas researchers took some time to acknowledge their significance, though, banks and financial market players were quicker.

There are several causes for the growing importance, sudden visibility and global relevance of SWFs in this phase.

1. The considerable growth of their assets following the increase in the price of oil (and of natural gas and raw materials), which rose from US$60 a barrel in August 2005 to US$147 on July 11 2008, as well as the emerging exporting markets' growing accumulation of significant currency reserves, a trend which had already begun in the preceding phase.

2. The increase in the number of SWFs, with a concentrated group taking shape in emerging markets. In this period 19 SWFs out of 53 were established. To cite the most important in terms of asset size: China Investment Corporation in 2007; the two Russian funds in 2008 deriving from the split of their forerunner, the Stabilization Fund of the Russian Federation; the Libyan Investment Authority in 2006; Qatar Investment Authority in 2005; the Investment Corporation of Dubai in 2006; Korea Investment Corporation in 2005; Bahrain

Mumtalakat in 2006 and the Chilean Economic and Social Stabilization Fund in 2007.

3.   The activism of SWFs in terms of international investment, particularly accentuated from the beginning of 2007 to mid-2008, with two-thirds of all transactions undertaken by SWFs registered in the period 1995 to mid-2008[10]. The increasing average size of the deals, and the astonishing total amount invested in this period, contributed to rising concern.

4.   The shift from west to east and from developed to emerging countries in the geoeconomic and political global balance of power.

5.   The tendency of SWFs to maintain secrets. Their opacity has in fact been one of the reasons for major concern.

6.   The entry into the game of Russian and Chinese SWFs. Since these funds belong to non-democratic, non-allied world powers, they triggered particular worries of a geopolitical nature in the US and Europe.

7.   The fact that SWFs represent a form of state capitalism in which decision-making mechanisms and investment time-horizons are different from those of the dominant (prior to the crisis) laissez-faire economic policies. As anyone knows, the excesses of freeing the market from rules has lost much credibility over the last two years, generating a revival of governments' economic role in developed countries as well.

Along with these factors, we should also consider two macro trends which characterise the destination of investments by SWFs.

One trend is geoeconomic in nature: the SWFs which first invested mainly in Asia turned towards the European Union and the United States. In dollars, from 1994 to 2004, SWFs invested just under US$15 billion in Asia and less than US$1 billion elsewhere. In 2008, up until October only US$3.5 billion was destined for Asia, US$11 billion to the EU, US$30 billion to the United States and US$1.5 billion to other countries. This shift also explains why, especially in 2007, SWFs leapt to the attention of the European Union and the United States: in less than two years, about US$26 billion was invested in the EU, and US$64 billion in the United States[11].

The other macro trend is sectoral, with the distinct preference of SWFs in 2007 and 2008 for the banking and financial sector. In just the first quarter of 2008, SWFs spent US$58 billion in Western financial institutions[12]. For the whole year, investments in the financial sector represented 96% of the total value. The surge of the financial sector is a recent phenomenon: in 2006 this sector attracted less than one fifth of SWF investment and still less in previous years. There are various reasons for sectoral imbalance in the activity of SWFs: expectations of formidable profits following those the sector had generated in the years 2000-2006; reputedly cheap share prices in 2007 and 2008 (in fact the market value of many large banks fell by 20-60% in just 18 months); the sector's strategic role; and pressures from Western institutions and financial operators to bail-out Western banks.

This table lists the main investments by SWFs in Western banks in the period 2006 to mid-2008.

Table 1 – Main investments in Western banks (2006 to mid-2008)

Date	SWF	Target	Value ($ million)
27 Mar 2006	Temasek	Standard Chartered	4,000
06 Oct 2006	Istithmar	Standard Chartered	1,000
23 Jul 2007	Temasek	Barclays	2,000
27 Nov 2007	ADIA	Citigroup	7,500
10 Dec 2007	GIC	UBS	9,760
19 Dec 2007	CIC	Morgan Stanley	5,000
27 Dec 2007	Temasek	Merrill Lynch	4,400
15 Jan 2008	GIC	Citigroup	6,880
15 Jan 2008	KIC	Merrill Lynch	2,000
15 Jan 2008	KIA	Merrill Lynch	2,000
16 Jan 2008	KIA	Citigroup	3,000
28 Jan 2008	QIA	Credit Suisse	3,000
8 Feb 2008	GIC	UBS	14,400
25 Jun 2008	QIA	Barclays	3,500
27 Jul 2008	Temasek	Merrill Lynch	3,400

Source: Bortolotti, Fotak, Megginson and Miracky (2009); Financial Times.

Finally, we should also consider the behaviour of the institutional, national and supranational recipients of SWFs. There are three distinct trends in this regard.

The first emerged in 2007, when various governments expressed concern and caution about SWF investments, specifically their investments in strategically sensitive companies. Several developed countries introduced or revitalised prudential regulations. There are at least two reasons for this reaction: the need to have transparent, market-driven investors; and for political reasons, since many SWFs are established in non-democratic countries.

The second trend took shape in the second half of 2008 as the financial crisis progressed. At this point the desire emerged in various countries to have SWFs as investors: to this end, heads of governments and ministries sent missions to countries with SWFs to incentivise these investments. From "barbarians" they became lenders of last resort for the shaky financial sector. Given their orientation to long-term instead of short-term capital gains, they initially helped mitigate the crisis of international financial markets, contributing to recapitalising Western banks in particular.

The third trend, which overlapped time-wise with the previous two, regarded international institutions and the European Union. In 2008 the European Commission set down guidelines for SWFs. Then the IMF, in agreement with the SWFs, launched voluntary regulations (the so-called Generally Accepted Principles and Practices (GAPP) or Santiago Principles, which we will discuss in greater detail in the last chapter) to ensure that the funds operated as fair market players.

From numbering 17 before 1997, in 2004 there were 34 SWFs and by 2008 there were 53. They went from the level of managed assets of US$500 billion in 1995 to nearly US$900 billion in 2004, and from there to an amount of total assets of between US$3,300 and US$4,000 billion (this figure fluctuates according to the estimates adopted) at the end of 2008[13].

From End-2008 Onwards: Reshaping Strategies

Since August-September 2008, the investment activity of SWFs has slowed for four reasons:

1. losses accumulated over the last year mainly from shareholdings in the US and European banking and financial sectors

2. the fall in the price of oil which went down from US$147 a barrel on July 11 2008 to US$40 a barrel at the end of December 2008, to recover to almost $80 by December 2009

3. the global recession, which contributed to shrinking Asian exporters' current account surpluses and levelling global imbalances

4. the risk in the home economies of SWFs due to the worldwide financial crisis.

The investments of SWFs in Citigroup, Barclays, Credit Suisse, UBS, Morgan Stanley and Merrill Lynch generated losses in value ranging between 60% and 90%[14]. These losses, mostly unrealised, were partially absorbed in 2009. Even if they have never been completely disclosed, according to some estimates they exceeded US$57 billion as of March 2009[15]. Thus the crisis hit SWFs very hard. They and the rest of the world discovered that they were not unbeatable, nor able to escape the financial storm.

In addition, SWFs were asked to provide support to domestic markets. Most countries in difficulty used their excess resources to tap budget deficits or provide stimulus packages, supporting domestic markets and institutions (Russia, Ireland, Kuwait, Qatar, UAE).

In 2009, the value of assets held by SWFs fluctuated, according to our estimates, between US$3,200 and US$3,800 billion.

After a period of retrenchment and a slowdown of investment activity, SWFs like many other investors used this break to rethink the structure and allocation of their portfolios and to adapt investment strategies to the changed financial scenario. The possible long-term challenges entailed a review of reserve levels versus SWF assets, redefining the proper level of asset diversification, changes in risk-management policies and targets, and increased scope for more active corporate governance. Moreover the new investment strategies of SWFs had to take into account the long-term development needs of their own countries and regions, their economic diversification and technological progress. Indeed, SWFs are increasingly subject to the scrutiny of domestic public opinion.

The image of SWFs has constantly changed and they have had to quickly adapt to changing circumstances. They are not, as said, enemies or saviours; they are investors with a strong and lasting influence on financial markets. While it is legitimate to ask them to be more transparent, a symmetrical request must be addressed to other financial actors such as hedge funds, private equity and investment banks if the mistake of using double standards is to be avoided. After the adoption of the Santiago Principles and the establishment of the International Forum of Sovereign Wealth Funds (IFSWF), SWFs seem willing to assume the role of responsible investors more involved in shaping the financial and monetary global framework. This is good news for the international community.

2.

What Are Sovereign Wealth Funds?

Defining Sovereign Wealth Funds

There are various definitions of SWFs which differ in terms of breadth but have common elements. Here we will consider the definition given by the IMF in the document containing the so-called Santiago Principles[16] (which will be covered in more depth in Chapter 7). In our opinion, this is the most authoritative definition, as it was agreed on with SWF representatives.

According to this definition, SWFs are:

> *special purpose investment funds or arrangements that are owned by the general government. Created by the general government for macroeconomic purposes, SWFs hold, manage, or administer assets to achieve financial objectives, and employ a set of investment strategies that include investing in foreign financial assets. SWFs have diverse legal, institutional, and governance structures. They are a heterogeneous group, comprising fiscal stabilisation funds, savings funds, reserve investment corporations, development funds, and pension reserve funds without explicit pension liabilities[17].*

SWFs derive their funds from balance of payments surpluses, official foreign currency operations, the proceeds of privatisations, fiscal surpluses, and receipts from commodity exports.

The IMF's definition excludes official reserves held by central banks, state-owned enterprises (SOEs) in the traditional sense, privately held and managed financial activities, and public and private pension funds which directly dispense pension benefits and are financed with pension contributions.

To better circumscribe the nature of these entities and to apply any national and supranational regulations, based on existing academic studies we can identify some of the distinctive features that differentiate SWFs from other entities or funds.

1. Sovereign wealth funds must be owned by a sovereign state, a definition which includes central governments as well as subnational entities. The latter allows us to include under the category of subnational the SWFs of the federal states of Alaska, Wyoming, New Mexico and Alabama in the United States, that of the province of Alberta in Canada and the Emirates of the United Arab Emirates. According to the main classifications, these are considered SWFs for all intents and purposes.

2. The portfolios of SWFs contain investments denominated in foreign currency, albeit not necessarily the majority or the total, thus excluding wholly national funds. This element does not exclude funds such as Singapore's Temasek and Malaysia's Khazanah. These funds, while still managing huge domestic investments, have part of their activities located abroad, and this has grown in recent years. However, this criterion does exclude, for example, Taiwan's fund, since its investments are exclusively domestic (to help stabilise national stock markets), and France's recently established Strategic Investment Fund (SIF), founded essentially to protect national industry from foreign buy-outs.

3. SWFs are characterised by the absence of short-term withdrawals (for example for pension obligations) and by long-term investment horizons. Usually they also have a low level of indebtedness, but in spite of their low financial leverage, it is still true that many of these funds are authorised to invest and do invest in private equity or hedge funds, as well as other highly indebted financial institutions, thus increasing their implicit level of financial leverage. In addition many funds, especially the most recent ones, are making a more aggressive use of leverage. Therefore, the absence of indebtedness will not be considered an essential element in classifying SFWs.

4. SWFs must be separate from central banks' official reserves and are managed with different criteria, preferring yields to liquidity and accepting higher levels of risk. This element could exclude some funds from SWFs, such as those managed

by the Saudi monetary authority (SAMA), the Chinese SAFE Investment Company, and the Hong Kong Monetary Authority's Investment Portfolio. Nevertheless, although these funds belong to the monetary authorities of those respective countries, they are managed separately from the central banks' official reserves, and can thus pursue investment strategies based on long-term horizons and higher risk propensity.

5. The search for yields above the risk-free rate. In some cases this is unavoidable for SWFs. Some funds are based on the transfer of currency assets from central banks' official reserves, for which the government pays an indebtedness cost linked to the need to issue bonds for sterilisation purposes (see the case of CIC). In this case the SWF's revenue should at least exceed the financing cost of the capital. Beyond these cases, SWFs need to invest in activities capable of producing long-term, risk-balanced returns to be consistent with their goals.

For reasons of simplicity, in this book we will also consider assets owned by governments and any administrative entities/authorities assigned to manage them as sovereign wealth funds. This applies, for example, to the Kuwait Investment Authority, which is not a fund but an investment company that manages two separate funds.

Finally, it is worthwhile defining so-called Sovereign Wealth Enterprises (SWEs); investment vehicles owned and controlled by SWFs. These are established to allow SWFs greater flexibility of movement, as well as to make them even less transparent. For simplicity, when we refer to investments and assets held by sovereign funds, we will also include those pertaining to SWEs without differentiating between them.

How SWFs Differ From Other Investment Entities

To better describe the nature of SWFs we will consider some of the ways in which they differ from other funds or investment entities.

In terms of public investment, SWFs are complementary to central banks' official reserves, pension funds and state-owned companies, but they are different from each of them.

One of the most important differences between SWFs and official reserves is the fact that SWFs, unlike reserves, needn't be 100% denominated in foreign currency, nor necessarily be invested in liquid assets such as cash, gold or public debt securities. SWFs do not have these prudential operating constraints and can thus afford higher exposure to risk as well as longer time horizons. As SWFs are not considered official reserves, they are not subject to the principles and rules of the international financial system, mainly determined by the IMF as far as transparency and consistency in complying with two main voluntary monitoring mechanisms: the Currency Composition of Official Foreign Exchange Reserves (COFER) and the Data Template on International Reserves and Foreign Currency Liquidity.

SWFs also differ from other public investments, such as corporations in which the state holds controlling shares (state-owned enterprises or SOEs). SOEs are mainly found in sectors such as energy, aeronautics, infrastructure, transport, telecommunications and utilities – i.e. those considered strategic for economic, social and public safety reasons. This distinction, while obvious in theory, is less clear in reality; these two forms of sovereign wealth often overlap and in practice are managed interchangeably by some governments.

In addition, SWFs differ from other types of investment funds such as hedge funds or private equity funds not only because the latter are private. While they do have some common features, such as the fact that they are not very transparent in their operations and are not strictly regulated, there are other important differences between these classes of investors. Whereas hedge funds are very highly leveraged, with a propensity for high risk, short-term return, SWFs feature a low level of debt (even though, as shown, they then invest in hedge funds and implicitly increase their leverage), less risk propensity (although the risk-propensity of SWFs is higher than that of official reserves and pension funds), and medium- to long-term horizons. Whereas with hedge funds and private equity funds, incentives can be aligned between ownership and management – for example, through the distribution of stock options – SWFs, because they are publicly owned and managed by bureaucrats with incentives that are not likely to be aligned with those of the fund, are subject to conflicts of interest and a series of problems related to governance. In the end, the shareholders of SWFs – i.e. the citizens of the owner state – often have no access to information on the management of sovereign wealth funds, whereas hedge funds normally feature higher standards of transparency, at least for partners and/or investors.

The most problematic distinction is with pension funds, and in particular public pension funds. Here we must specify which pension funds we are dealing with. According to the OECD[18], it is useful to differentiate normal public pension funds that belong to the national social security system – social security reserve funds (SSRF) – from sovereign pension reserve funds (SPRF).

With SSRFs, inflows derive from employees' or employers' pension contributions and they periodically distribute pension benefits. SPRFs, on the other hand, are established by governments as autonomous entities separate from the national social-security systems, and their inflows are direct fiscal transfers by the government, aimed at coping with future deficits of the pension system even if they do not imply direct liabilities to pensioners.

Whereas SWFs differ significantly from the first type (SSRFs), differences between SWFs and SPRFs are much more subtle. The funding for pension funds of the first type (SSRF) comes from contributions paid in for pension purposes, rather than currency or fiscal surpluses. SSRF pension funds require sufficient liquidity for periodic payments to beneficiaries, but SWFs do not have this burden. SSRF pension funds are transparent in terms of their financial operations and goals, while SWFs are often not transparent. Pension funds may be completely denominated in domestic currency; SWFs must invest, at least part of their funds, in foreign currency, according to the definition provided earlier. With SPRFs, the differences are less marked. For both SPRFs and SWFs, funding comes from the government and specifically from currency and/or fiscal surpluses. Since SPRF-type pension funds do not have explicit liabilities to pay out to pensioners on a periodic basis, they are more similar to SWFs than to SSRFs.

Based on these considerations it is unclear whether, in view of the similarities, SPRFs can somehow be assimilated as SWFs and treated homogeneously (as well as in terms of applying codes of conduct). Edwin Truman[19] includes both SSRFs and SPRFs in his classification.

The IMF[20], on the other hand, proposes excluding SSRFs from the definition of SWFs, and instead includes SPRFs. We essentially agree with the latter approach. Thus in classifying the sovereign funds which follow, we will include SPRF-type pension funds like the Norwegian Government Pension Fund – Global, China's National Social Security, France's Fonds de Réserve pour les Retraites, Australia's Future Fund, Ireland's National Pensions Reserve Fund, New Zealand's Superannuation Fund and Chile's pension fund but we will not include, for example, California's CalPERS or the Japanese or Canadian pension funds.

Where Do Their Financial Resources Come From?

SWFs are classified according to two main criteria: the first is where the financial resources come from; the second is what goals are being pursued. There are two types of SWFs according to the first criterion.

1. Commodity funds, which derive their financial resources from the export of raw materials (mostly petroleum) owned by the state or from taxes/royalties related to their sale. Commodity SWFs often but not always benefit from revenues generated by the scarcity of raw materials, possibly accentuated by the existence of a cartel between producer countries. The most important funds of this type are concentrated in the Middle East, Norway and Russia.

2. Non-commodity funds, which get their financial resources from non-energy current account and other balance-of-payments surpluses accumulated by some countries, in particular Asian ones and especially China, as well as from privatisation revenues and other fiscal proceeds. In such situations it has been stated that a sort of quasi-rent is being generated by a series of asymmetries (for example in the currency exchange rate), which affects international competition. However, these types of practices have often been adopted by developed countries in the phases of accelerated growth during which they 'emerged'. The most important funds of this type are Asian and belong to the governments of China and Singapore.

Commodity funds represent the majority of assets behind SWFs, nearly two-thirds (60%) of the total.

What is Their Purpose and How Do They Differ From Each Other?

SWFs have multiple goals: to protect and stabilise the national economy from volatility in the prices of raw materials and exports; to diversify sources of national wealth; to increase financial returns of official reserves; to diversify holdings of an excessive quantity of securities denominated in dollars; to encourage the accumulation of savings for future generations in anticipation of exhausting raw materials; and to finance economic and social development in the home country.

The IMF classifies SWFs based on their goals, identifying five types.

1. Stabilisation funds, with the primary purpose of stabilising and insulating fiscal policies from fluctuations in the prices of raw materials.

2. Savings funds, with the goal of converting non-renewable resources into financial wealth for the benefit of future generations and redistributing the proceeds from natural resources among generations as fairly as possible.

3. Reserve investment corporations, the assets of which can be counted as official reserves, but which in contrast to official reserves, are managed separately and can be utilised in more profitable investments.

4. Development funds, with the scope of financing socio-economic development projects or promoting specific industrial policies.

5. Pension reserve funds, which by utilising sources other than normal pension schemes, have the goal of coping with pension indebtedness (those previously defined as sovereign pension reserve funds, or SPRF).

The distinctions between these funds should not be seen as rigid, in that a SWF can have multiple goals or may be established with certain objectives that change over time.

When we intersect the origin of funds with their purpose we can deduce the following pattern: commodity SWFs tend to be stabilisation or savings funds; reserve investment corporations tend to be the non-commodity type; and development and pension funds belong to both types.

The diversity of objectives implies different investment time horizons, different risk-profit trade-offs and therefore different asset management strategies. For example, stabilisation funds are more liquid with shorter-term horizons, whereas savings funds are less liquid with longer time horizons.

In addition to different objectives, SWFs have varying legal statuses. SWFs may be set up under specific laws, national budget acts, and in some cases a country's constitution provides for their creation. They may be set up under a separate legal status from that of the government or the central bank, but they may also remain in a pool of assets owned by the government or by the monetary authority. SWFs belonging to the latter category are generally controlled by the ministry of finance and managed by one of its agencies or the central bank. The law defines how they are financed and how to access them, which also depends on their purpose. Financing may be based on surpluses from the prices of raw materials compared to predefined targets (stabilisation funds), may depend on specific fixed objectives for the fund (pension funds), or can be discretional. The rules for withdrawal may be based on whether or not there is a budget deficit or special public financing needs, on prices of raw materials sinking below predefined targets (stabilisation funds), on current account deficits, or on calculations of future liabilities (pension funds).

It is therefore evident that SWFs are a non-homogeneous category of financial player, characterised by highly differentiated legal and institutional status, declared and pursued objectives, and strategies and operating modes on international financial markets.

A Possible League Table

In this section we provide a league table of sovereign funds by size of assets based on various sources. 53 SWFs are shown in Table 2, with certain qualification coordinates such as country of origin, estimated value of assets, year of establishment, origin of financial resources (C stands for commodity and NC for non-commodity).

The latest available data is provided for each SWF. Therefore reference periods may be different from one fund to another (mainly spanning December 2008 to September 2009) and are reported in the notes.

Table 2 – Sovereign wealth funds in order of asset size (US$ billion), values or range (latest data available). Notes are expanded in *Notes on data*. Table continued overleaf. C = Commodity, NC = Non-commodity.

Country	Name	Assets (US$ billion)	Year established	Type
UAE	Abu Dhabi Investment Authority (ADIA)	282-627[1]	1976	C
Norway	Norwegian Government Pension Fund – Global	431[2]	1990	C
Saudi Arabia	Various funds belonging to Saudi Arabian Monetary Agency (SAMA)	365[3]	-	C
China	SAFE Investment Company	300[4]	1997	NC
China	China Investment Corporation	298[5]	2007	NC
Singapore	Government Investment Corporation (GIC)	180-248[6]	1981	NC
Kuwait	Kuwait Investment Authority (KIA)	169-228[7]	1953	C
China/Hong Kong	Hong Kong Monetary Authority – Investment Portfolio	140[8]	1998	NC
Singapore	Temasek Holdings	119[9]	1974	NC
China	National Social Security Fund	114[10]	2000	NC
Russia	National Wealth Fund	93[11]	2008	C
Russia	Reserve Fund	75[12]	2008	C

Country	Name	Assets (US$ billion)	Year established	Type
Libya	Libyan Investment Authority	65-70[13]	2006	C
Qatar	Qatar Investment Authority (QIA)	58-65[14]	2005	C
Australia	Australian Government Future Fund (AGFF)	59[15]	2006	NC
UAE	Investment Corporation of Dubai (ICD)	20-82[16]	2006	C
Algeria	Revenue Regulation Fund	47[17]	2000	C
France	Fonds de Réserve pour les Retraites	47[18]	2001	NC
USA	Alaska Permanent Fund Corporation (APRF)	34[19]	1976	C
Ireland	National Pensions Reserve Fund (NPRF)	32[20]	2001	NC
Brunei	Brunei Investment Agency (BIA)	30[21]	1983	C
Kazakhstan	Kazakhstan National Fund (KNF)	26[22]	2000	C
Iran	Oil Stabilization Fund	13-38[23]	1999	C
South Korea	Korea Investment Corporation (KIC)	25[24]	2005	NC
Malaysia	Khazanah Nasional Berhad (KNB)	20-25[25]	1993	NC
UAE	Mubadala Development Company – Abu Dhabi	22[26]	2002	C
Nigeria	Excess Crude Oil Account	9-20[27]	2004	C
Canada	Alberta's Heritage Fund	14.5[28]	1976	C
Bahrain	Mumtalakat Holding Company	14[29]	2006	C
UAE	Abu Dhabi – International Petroleum Investment Company (IPIC)	14[30]	1984	C
USA	New Mexico State Investment Office Trust Fund	13[31]	1958	NC
Chile	Economic and Social Stabilization Fund (ESSF)	12.6[32]	2007	C

Country	Name	Assets (US$ billion)	Year established	Type
New Zealand	New Zealand Superranuation Fund	11.2[33]	2003	NC
Azerbaijan	State Oil Fund (SOFAZ)	10.9[34]	1999	C
UAE	Istithmar World (Dubai World)	9[35]	2003	C
Brazil	Sovereign Fund of Brazil	8.6[36]	2009	NC
Oman	State General Reserve Fund	8.2[37]	1980	C
Botswana	Pula Fund	6.6[38]	1966	C
Saudi Arabia	Sanabil al-Saudia (Public Investment Fund)	5.3[39]	2008	C
Timor-Leste	Timor-Leste Petroleum Fund	4.9[40]	2005	C
USA	Permanent Wyoming Mineral Trust Fund (PWMTF)	4.3[41]	1974	C
Chile	Pension Reserve Fund	3.5[42]	2006	C
USA	Alabama Trust Fund	2.6[43]	1986	C
Trinidad and Tobago	Heritage and Stabilization Fund	2.4[44]	2000	C
UAE	RAK Investment Authority	1.2[45]	2005	C
Venezuela	FEM – Macroeconomic Stabilization Fund	0.8[46]	1998	C
Vietnam	State Capital Investment Corporation (SCIC)	0.5[47]	2006	NC
Kiribati	Revenue Equalization Reserve Fund	0.4[48]	1957	C
Indonesia	Government Investment Unit	0.34[49]	2006	NC
Mauritania	National Fund for Hydrocarbon Reserves	0.3[50]	2006	C
Mexico	Oil Revenues Stabilisation Fund	NA	2000	C
Oman	Oman Investment Fund	NA	2006	C
UAE	Emirates Investment Authority	NA	2007	C
TOTAL ASSETS		3,222-3,809		

Notes on data

Sources: Authors' elaboration from annual reports and latest web-based information provided by SWFs when available as specified in the notes. When not available, indirect sources as specified below have been used.

[1] Lower bound is from Miracky and Bortolotti (2009), as of December 2008; upper bound is from SWF Institute accessed January 2010. Setser and Ziemba (2009), estimate (US$328 billion) is included in this range.

[2] Norges Bank Investment Management (NBIM) (2009). The amount includes only the assets of the Government Pension Fund and excludes other funds managed by NBIM.

[3] Ziemba (2009). This amount includes also foreign currency activities of government pension funds managed by Sama, whereas the official reserves of the Saudi central bank are not included.

[4] China Investment Corporation (2008).

[5] Lower bound is from Miracky and Bortolotti (2009) and Hoguet, Nugée and Rozanov (2009); upper bound is from SWF Institute accessed January 2010. They all refer to December 2008.

[6] Lower bound is from Hoguet, Nugée and Rozanov (2009); upper bound is from Miracky and Bortolotti (2009), as of December 2008 and SWF Institute accessed January 2010.

[7] Lower bound is from Miracky and Bortolotti (2009), as of December 2008 and from Kern (2009); upper bound is from Setser and Ziemba (2009). Hoguet, Nugée and Rozanov (2009), as of February 2009, and SWF Institute accessed January 2010 provide an estimate (US$202 billion) that is included in this range.

[8] SWF Institute accessed January 2010. This amount refers to 31 August 2009 and includes only assets of the Investment Portfolio, one of the two funds that make up the Exchange Fund owned by the HK Monetary Authority. The second fund, the Backing Portfolio used to support monetary policy, is not included.

[9] Temasek Holdings as at 31 July 2009 – Institutional website: www.temasekholdings.com.sg/about_us.htm

[10] China National Social Security Fund, Institutional website, total assets as at December 2009: www.ssf.gov.cn

[11] Ministry of Finance of the Russian Federation, institutional website, as at 01/12/2009, available at: www1.minfin.ru/en/nationalwealthfund

[12] Ministry of Finance of the Russian Federation, institutional website, as at 01/12/2009, available at: www1.minfin.ru/en/reservefund

[13] Lower bound is from Miracky and Bortolotti (2009), as of December, 2008; upper bound is from SWF Institute accessed January 2010 and from Hoguet, Nugée and Rozanov (2009), as of December 2008.

[14] Lower bound is from Setser and Ziemba (2009), as of December 2008; upper bound is from SWF Institute accessed January 2010.

[15] Australia Future Fund – institutional website as of 30 September 2009: www.futurefund.gov.au

[16] Lower bound is from SWF Institute accessed January 2010; upper bound is from Miracky and Bortolotti (2009), as of December 2008 and from Kern (2009).

[17] SWF Institute accessed January 2010; Kern (2009).

[18] Fonds des Réserves pour le Retraites, institutional website, Press Release 26 October 2009 – accessed on 30 September 2009, available at www.fondsdereserve.fr

[19] Alaska Permanent Fund (2009).

[20] National Pensions Reserve Fund – NTMA (2009).

[21] Miracky and Bortolotti (2009), as of December 2008; SWF Institute accessed January 2010; Hoguet, Nugée and Rozanov (2009).

[22] National Fund of the Republic of Kazakhstan, institutional website, as of 1 September 2009: www.minfin.kz/structure/data

[23] Lower bound is from SWF Institute accessed January 2010; upper bound is from Hoguet, Nugée and Rozanov (2009), as of December 2008.

[24] Korea Investment Corporation – institutional website – fact sheet section – AUM as of December 2008: www.kic.go.kr/en/?mid=rl06

[25] Lower bound is from Hoguet, Nugée and Rozanov (2009); upper bound is from SWF Institute accessed January 2010. Miracky and Bortolotti (2009), provide an intermediate estimate (US$23 billion) as of December 2008.

[26] Mubadala Development Company (2009), at 30 June 2009.

[27] Lower bound is from SWF Institute accessed January 2010; upper bound is from Hoguet, Nugée and Rozanov (2009), as of March 2009.

[28] Government of Alberta (2009), update as of 30 September 2009.

[29] Mumtalakat institutional website – CEO Annual Report 31 December 2007: www.bmhc.bh/investor/ceo.asp

[30] International Petroleum Investment Company, institutional website: www.ipic.ae/En/Menu/index.aspx?MenuID=3&CatID=6&mnu=Cat

[31] New Mexico State Investment Council (2009).

[32] Chile's Ministry of Finance – Fondo de Estabilización Económica y Social – Monthly Report 30 November 2009: www.dipres.cl/572/articles-58452_doc_pdf.pdf

[33] New Zealand Superannuation Fund, institutional website – Portfolio Update to 30 November 2009: www.nzsuperfund.co.nz/files/Performance_to_30_November_2009.pdf

[34] SOFAZ, Institutional website – Revenue and Expenditure Statement for January-March 2009 – assets at 1 April 2009: www.oilfund.az/en/news/189

[35] Miracky and Bortolotti (2009), as of December 2008. Since Dubai World is almost completely opaque and it is impossible to get an estimate of the size of its assets under management, we consider in this table only Istithmar World owned 100% by Dubai World. We are aware that it would have been more correct to report Dubai World's assets and that the figure reported in the table represents only a small fraction of the total of Dubai World's assets.

[36] SWF Institute accessed January 2010.

[37] SWF Institute accessed January 2010; Miracky and Bortolotti (2009), as of December 2008.

[38] International Forum of Sovereign Wealth Funds, IFSWF, Members information on Pula Fund, assets under management at the end of 2007: www.ifswf.org/members-info.htm

[39] SWF Institute accessed January 2010; Hoguet, Nugée and Rozanov (2009), as of April 2009.

[40] International Forum of Sovereign Wealth Funds, IFSWF, members information on Timor Leste Petroleum Fund, assets under management as of June 2009: www.ifswf.org/members-info.htm

[41] Wyoming Treasurer's Office (2009).

[42] Chile's Ministry of Finance – Fondo de Reserva de Pensiones – Monthly Report 30 November 2009: www.minhda.cl/fondos_soberanos/fondo_de_reserva_info_valor.php

[43] Kay Ivey Alabama State Treasurer, Report at 30 September 2009: www.treasury.state.al.us/Content/Documents/Alabama%20Trust%20Fund%20101.pdf

[44] International Forum of Sovereign Wealth Funds, IFSWF, members information on Trinidad and Tobago Heritage Stabilization Fund, assets under management as of August 2008: www.ifswf.org/members-info.htm

[45] SWF Institute accessed January 2010; Miracky and Bortolotti (2009), as of December 2008.

[46] FEM, Institutional Website, Monthly Financial Detail as of November 2009: www.bcv.org.ve/fem/fem.asp

[47] SWF Institute accessed January 2010; Miracky and Bortolotti (2009), as of December 2008.

[48] SWF Institute accessed January 2010; Miracky and Bortolotti (2009), as of December 2008.

[49] SWF Institute accessed January 2010.

[50] SWF Institute accessed January 2010.

Given the lack of transparency of some SWFs, our estimates of assets should be considered only indicative and therefore treated with due caution. In some cases, especially when a fund does not make its data official, figures have been collected from various publicly available sources, and variation in estimates is such that it was not possible to identify a specific value. We therefore show both the extremes in the interval of variation, and for calculation and classification purposes we have used the averages of the intervals.

The data is the latest available. Since the availability of up-to-date figures varies from fund to fund, the asset values are not always aligned time-wise. In most cases we have obtained data from December 2008, and in some cases from the third-quarter 2009. In most cases data does incorporate the losses caused by the financial crisis. The two last SWFs, the Oman Investment Fund and the Emirates Investment Authority, have been recently set up, and figures relating to the size of their assets are not available. For the Emirates Investment Authority, Monitor Group-FEEM reports a range varying between ten and 20 billion US$. However, for prudence, we chose not to report any data in accordance with the Sovereign Wealth Fund Institute. For the Mexican Oil Revenues Stabilization Fund we did not report any figure because the fund was depleted in 2008-2009 for budget needs and it is not clear what its remaining size is.

Terengganu Investment Authority, established in 2008 in Malaysia, has been expanded to a federal entity called 1Malaysia Development Bhd (1MDB) endowed with US$1 billion. We have not included it in our list since it is exclusively focused on investing in Malaysia, with the explicit aim of enhancing the development of the domestic economy.

At the same time, several countries have decided to establish their own SWFs. Equatorial Guinea has authorised the establishment of a Fund for Future. Turkmenistan has readied to launch a Stabilization Fund. Japan is planning to launch a SWF (whose endowment could reach US$100 billion) to invest its huge foreign exchange reserves. India is also considering establishing a SWF with an initial value of US$5 billion that will probably be managed by an independent entity to be set up by a parliamentary act. Brazil has already established its sovereign wealth fund and it has been included in Table 2 since it is ready to operate, even though it risks being partially depleted to finance public expenditure in case tax collection is not enough to avoid the widening of the budget deficit. (All this is as of the time of writing.)

According to our estimates[21], the managed assets of SWFs fluctuate between US$3,222 and US$3,809 billion. The average value is US$3,516 billion. Even after the financial crisis, the losses from which have been incorporated in most of the funds' estimates, their aggregate values remain solidly above US$3,000 billion. This is an impressive figure, especially if compared with the managed assets held up until the mid to late 2000s. Comparing this figure (early 2009) with one year before (early 2008), total managed assets have decreased from US$3,700[22] to US$3,516 billion, losing about 5% or US$190 billion. This synthetic figure hides quite different situations, since some funds have increased the value of their portfolios (for example, Norwegian Government Pension Fund, China Investment Corporation and China National Social Security Fund), others have remained almost stable (Libyan Investment Authority and Qatar Investment Authority), and others have lost ground (ADIA, Sama, Kuwait Investment Authority, the two funds from Singapore and the two funds from Russia).

To Which Countries Do They Belong?

In terms of geographic origin, 37% of total SWF assets are owned by Asian countries. Some of the most important Asian SWFs are Chinese, followed by Singapore's Government Investment Corporation (GIC) and Temasek. Other countries such as Brunei, Kazakhstan, South Korea, Malaysia, Azerbaijan, East Timor, Vietnam and Indonesia own quite small funds. In Asia, the lion's share of SWFs are non-commodity funds. Here the most important country is China, which in addition to the China Investment Corporation (CIC) owns the SAFE Investment Company, a subsidiary of the foreign exchange reserve corporation owned by the central bank, the Investment Portfolio of Hong Kong's Monetary Authority and the National Social Security Fund, an SPRF-type pension fund. All of these entities are funded by currency and fiscal surpluses and invest a significant portion of those resources abroad according to typical SWF strategies.

Figure 2 – The geographic origin of SWFs

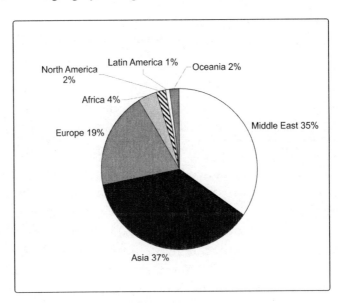

Source: Our elaborations on Table 2. Where asset values are expressed in terms of a range, we have considered their simple mean.

Until one year ago, the largest share of SWF assets was owned by Middle Eastern countries[23]. However, as foreseen by several analysts, Asian funds have rapidly caught up and today Middle Eastern countries only have around the same share of the world total (35%) as Asian ones. Not surprisingly, all of the Middle East's are commodity funds, specifically petroleum. The region's largest SWFs are the Abu Dhabi

Investment Authority (ADIA), the funds managed by the Saudi Arabian Monetary Agency, the Kuwait Investment Authority (KIA), the Qatar Investment Authority (QIA) plus several other funds belonging to the UAE. Funds owned by Iran, Bahrain and Oman also belong to this region. Estimates tend to be uncertain since the opacity of many of these SWFs makes it impossible to find out the actual amount of their assets; nor can we be certain to have assessed all of them, in view of many of these governments' reluctance to publish information on possible investment vehicles they own.

Next comes Europe, both EU and non-EU, representing 19% of SWFs in terms of assets held. Most of these assets consist of the Norwegian pension fund and the two Russian funds, the National Wealth Fund and the Reserve Fund, all of which are commodity-based funds. Europe here is meant in the geographical sense, since the EU is of marginal relevance (with only the French and Irish pension funds).

Africa represents 4% of total assets. The main funds are the Libyan Investment Authority and the Algerian Revenue Regulation Fund. These are obviously commodity funds, as are the other minor African funds belonging to Nigeria, Botswana and Mauritania.

The least significant areas are North America with 2% (here the Alaskan oil fund has the pre-eminent role, followed by the Canadian fund from Alberta, also oil-based), Oceania with 2% (essentially represented by pension funds from Australia and New Zealand, both of which are non-commodity funds) and Latin America with approximately 1%, with the most important one from Chile, commodity-based (originally founded with revenues from copper exports), and a recently established Brazilian non-commodity-based fund.

Two clarifications help to support the thesis on SWFs originating from rents or quasi-rents. First, at the end of 2008, Middle Eastern countries held 41% of the world's known natural gas reserves and 60% of petroleum reserves[24]. This tells us that they are in a position of natural rent. Secondly, China's current account surplus exceeded US$420 billion at the end of 2008, or 9.8% of the country's GDP[25], and Chinese reserves, the highest in the world, were approximately US$2,399 billion in December 2009[26]. Year-on-year growth rates of Asian reserves until

2008 (31%) and Middle Eastern ones (35%) boosted the rate of growth of global reserves (27%), especially considering that the equivalent growth rate for industrialised countries was less than 8%.

Comparisons With Other Major Economic-Financial Variables

The managed assets of SWFs fluctuate between US$3,222 and US$3,809 billion. These are remarkable amounts since they represent:

- almost 6% of global GDP (US$60,917 billion in 2008[27])

- about 10% of the capitalisation of world stock markets (US$33,513 billion in 2008[28])

- more than 4% of total public and private debt securities (US$83,530 billion in 2008[29])

- 3.6% of total bank assets (US$97,381 billion in 2008[30])

- 1.6% of the total of all global financial assets (including bonds, equities and bank assets) at the end of 2008, estimated at US$214,424 billion[31]

- half the total (50.7%) currency reserves held by central banks (US$6,909 billion at December, 2008[32]).

If these fractions seem significant, they become even more so when comparing the value of SWFs to:

- the GDP of emerging markets at the end of 2008 (US$20,606 billion[33]), of which SWFs represent 17%

- total financial assets (including bonds, equities and bank assets) exchanged on emerging financial markets (US$34,394 billion at the end of 2008[34]), of which SWFs represent 10%.

Figure 3 – SWFs in comparison with other economic-financial variables (US$ trillion, year 2008)

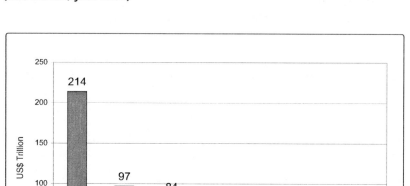

Source: Our elaborations on IMF (2009); IMF, World Economic Outlook Database, 2009; IMF, COFER, 2009; Table 2.

If we compare SWF assets to those of other financial actors such as insurance companies (US$21 trillion[35]) and pension funds (US$19 trillion[36]), SWFs represent respectively 17% and 18% of them. Compared to hedge funds (about US$1.3 trillion[37]), SWFs are about two and a half times as large.

One important difference to remember when comparing SWFs to these categories of investors is the fact that while the latter have thousands of operators, the assets of SWFs are concentrated in just a few entities. The largest five SWFs represent about half of total assets and the largest ten hold 74% of them. The main SWFs manage portfolios of the size of the largest private investors, with the difference that SWFs are generally less indebted. The concentration of assets and power in the hands of a few actors, especially considering their sovereign nature, is one of the reasons SWFs initially caused concerns among recipient countries.

Figure 4 – SWFs compared to other investors (US$ trillion, year 2008)

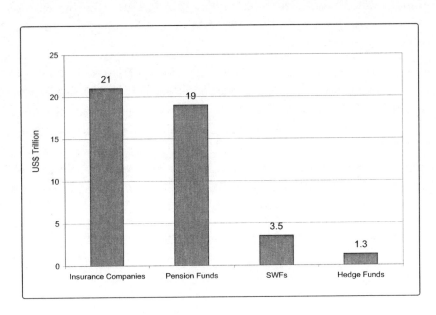

Source: Our elaborations on Kern (2009) and on Table 2.

Growth Forecasts

Considering the weight of SWFs in the economic and financial landscape and the attention they have attracted so far, forecasts of their growth are significant and should be monitored. The financial turmoil of 2008 can be considered a watershed. Until that time very optimistic projections circulated. Recent events, however, have triggered a major reversal in outlook, inducing more caution. We will therefore present both sets of forecasts in order to better understand the significance of the turnabout.

Pre-crisis forecasts

In the forecast scenario up to mid-2008 there was widespread belief that SWF assets would grow strongly in the coming years. According to Jen[38], SWF assets could have reached US$12,000 billion by 2015. This estimate was based on the assumption that SWFs would have nominal annual returns of 5.5% and they would grow not only in terms of returns but also due to inflows of surplus financial resources in the SWF home countries, with their economies also forecast to grow strongly. On this basis, Jen estimated that SWFs would have also exceeded official reserves by 2011.

An alternative hypothesis by Kern[39] foresaw SWF assets growing as follows: in a prudential scenario they could have reached US$4.2 trillion by 2010 and US$7 trillion by 2015 (corresponding to an average annual growth rate of 11%); in an intermediate scenario, up to US$4.7 trillion by 2010 and US$10 trillion by 2015 (corresponding to an average annual growth rate of 15%); in an optimistic scenario, up to US$5 trillion by 2010 and US$14 trillion by 2015 (corresponding to an average annual growth rate of 22%).

Figure 5 – SWF growth scenarios (US$ trillion)

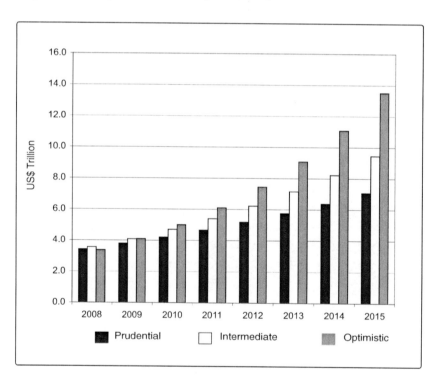

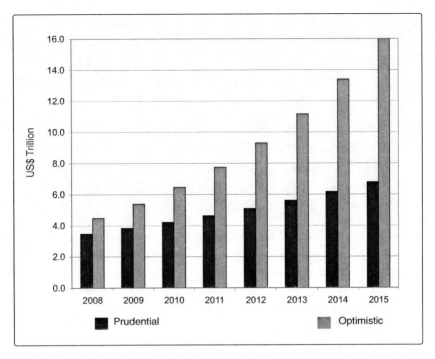

Source: Our elaborations on Kern (2008) and Fernandez and Eschweiler (2008).

According to JP Morgan's estimates[40], the growth rate of SWFs would have oscillated between 11% and 20%, with corresponding asset values in 2012 of between US$5,000 and US$9,300 billion depending on the chosen scenario. According to Standard Chartered[41], SWFs would have grown at almost 20% reaching US$13.4 trillion by 2017 in the best scenario, while in the worst case they would have grown to US$5.3 trillion.

The notable variation among estimates is due to the high level of uncertainty related to developments of three key factors which determine SWF growth:

1. volatility in the prices of raw materials and in particular the price of oil, which determines the size of commodity funds

2. trends in the current account balances of the major exporting countries (in particular Asian countries), which depend, among other factors, on global growth rates, growth rates of exporting countries, currency policies

adopted and prevalent exchange rates on the markets. This element is important because it affects currency reserves, which in turn determine the size of SWFs. In any case these countries' desire to transfer financial resources from reserves to SWFs is difficult to predict

3. yields on financial markets which determine the returns on activities managed by SWFs and therefore growth deriving from accumulation. SWF yields are difficult to estimate because of many funds' lack of transparency and also in light of the 2007-2009 financial crisis.

Since each of these points is subject to a high degree of uncertainty, and since available data on the current size of SWFs is also uncertain, most analysts have chosen to consider alternative scenarios.

Forecasts after the crisis

The financial turmoil of 2007-2009 caused many analysts to revise their forecasts. Each of the three elements mentioned in the previous section (price of oil, current account balances and financial market yields) was heavily affected by the crisis. We will now examine them in more detail.

Lower oil prices (which dropped from an average of US$100 a barrel in 2008 with a peak of US$147 in July to a low of US$34 in February 2009 and rebounded to almost US$80 at the end of the year) cut oil exporting countries' revenues and thus their foreign currency availability. With the price of oil fluctuating between US$35 and US$80 per barrel in 2009, current account balances in Middle Eastern countries shrank from US$345 billion in 2008 to US$43 billion in 2009[42], marking a significant reversal in comparison to the steep increase recorded until 2008. As a consequence, inflows to SWFs slowed down. However, oil prices were expected to stay at around US$70 in 2010 and current account balances of Middle Eastern countries were forecast to rise again to US$152 billion. Setser and Ziemba[43] estimate that, with oil at US$75 a barrel, the Gulf economies should be able to generate savings of around US$125-150 billion to pour into SWFs. On the contrary, if the oil price stayed at US$50, it is likely that the Gulf economies would tap into their reserves. Even in the best scenario of oil reaching US$100 per barrel over 2010-2015, the Gulf economies will pour savings again into SWFs, but these funds are unlikely to reach the optimistic figures forecasted before the crisis.

In Russia – in addition to the shrinking of the current account balance from US$102.4 billion in 2008 to US$45.5 billion in 2009 due to oil-price volatility – a weaker ruble, rising unemployment and the credit crisis all contributed to squeezing the value of national savings. SWFs were tapped to cover budget deficits.

Figure 6 – Current account balances for selected economies (US$ billion)

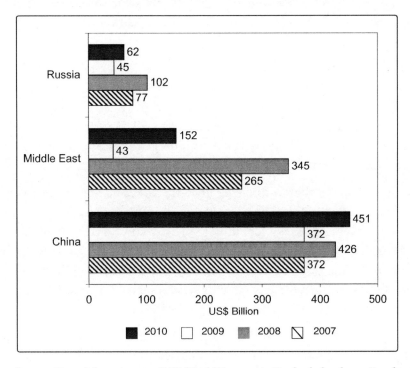

Source: Our elaborations on IMF, World Economic Outlook database, October 2009.

China's current account surplus exceeded US$420 billion at the end of 2008, or 9.8% of the country's GDP (in 2007 these figures were estimated at USD$372 billion or 11% of GDP)[44]. In 2009 it dropped to an estimated US$371.5 billion. This in turn tends to slow reserves accumulation and thus the resources available for SWFs. Chinese reserves, the highest in the world, increased from US$1,946 billion in

December 2008 to US$2,399 billion in December 2009[45], with a growth rate of 23.3%, lower than 27.4% in 2008 and 43.3% in 2007. They are one of the few countries whose rate of reserves growth continues to increase, albeit at a slower pace. It is also interesting to note in this regard that China secretly[46] increased its official gold reserves up to 1000 tons, which ranks this country sixth in the world. China has also increased gold extraction and in 2008 became the world's largest producer, overtaking South Africa. China's[47] (but also India's) interest in gold makes it clear that the increase in the price of gold, which has more than doubled in the last five years and is now over US$1,000/oz, could be a long term phenomenon of diversification of official reserves which will affect the reorganisation of the world monetary system if and when it is carried out.

Not only current accounts have suffered. Many emerging markets' reserves have also been used to compensate for capital flight and to avoid currency crises, creating the need to restore the official reserves used, thus again limiting future transfers to SWFs. After the crisis, a reversal in the preference towards building liquid and secure forex central bank reserves has indeed reappeared.

Another element that influences growth forecasts is the return on invested assets. From this point of view SWFs suffered shrinking balance sheets. Losses accumulated by many SWFs from their investments, especially in Western financial institutions, reduced their assets. According to our estimates, SWFs lost US$190 billion in one year in terms of managed assets. However, due to the opacity of many funds, this estimate must be treated with caution.

Finally, the need for expansive fiscal measures to counterbalance the recession caused many SWF home countries to be more inclined to use available resources for domestic purposes (rather than deploying them in investments abroad). Priorities shifted from accumulating savings and distributing wealth across generations to supporting short-term fiscal stimulus and financial sector rescues. In October 2008, SWFs from Qatar, Kuwait and Russia had to intervene in their own domestic financial markets to support the local economy and prevent stock markets from collapsing.

The financial crisis which hit the world, along with the real crisis which followed it, ensured that among all the possible scenarios outlined beforehand, the least optimistic ones became the most plausible.

Jen and Andreopoulos[48] reviewed their estimates and hypothesised more modest growth for SWFs and a slower accumulation of assets compared to what was calculated a year earlier. First of all they estimated that in 2008, taking into account their lack of transparency, SWFs incurred losses of 25% of their initial portfolios. The percentage of loss is derived from the (hypothetical) division of the funds' portfolios into 25% fixed income securities, 45% stocks and 30% alternative investments, and from the average losses of the indices of each of these categories. The 25% loss applied to the approximately US$3,000 billion in assets estimated by Jen at the beginning of 2008, thus reducing SWF assets at the end of 2008 to US$2,250 billion. To the losses already incurred they added the lower growth rates forecast for future years. The new forecasts go up to a maximum of US$9,700 billion of assets in 2015 compared to US$12,000 billion forecast a year and a half earlier. The two authors also reforecast the date for SWFs to exceed official reserves, moving it from 2011 to 2014.

Jen and Andreopoulos' new forecasts converge with those of Kern's intermediate scenario and also fit into a middle position compared to those of JP Morgan.

According to Subacchi[49] on the other hand, the total value of SWFs will not increase in 2009 and 2010 and their influence on global markets will consequently decrease. SWF total assets will struggle to reach between US$5 and 6 trillion by 2012.

According to Kern[50], in ten years (2009-2019) total SWF assets are likely to amount to US$7 trillion, more than doubling today's figures.

Volatility in commodity prices and possible turmoil on financial markets makes the projections uncertain. If macroeconomic imbalances at the source of SWFs resume their previous trend with widening US deficits and strong Chinese surpluses, SWFs will rebound. If, instead, those imbalances disappear, SWF inflows will stay low and their economic and political clout will remain subdued.

Economic recovery, especially in emerging economies, and the rise of oil and commodity prices along with an upswing in financial markets, with asset values in emerging countries rapidly inflating again, would mean that global macroeconomic imbalances would not change so much in future.

Therefore, the economic-financial and political weight of SWFs will continue to be important for their effects on financial markets; on currency markets, specifically due to the relationships between the dollar, euro, yen and emerging market currencies; and on stock markets due to the influence of their geographical, sectoral and corporate choices.

3.

The Most Representative Actors

L et us now consider the most representative SWFs in terms of assets, broken down per region and country.

For the Persian Gulf countries and Mediterranean Africa (corresponding to the Middle East and North Africa or MENA region) these are commodity funds such as Abu Dhabi's (the largest one), Kuwait's (the oldest), and Libya's (the most relevant in Africa). In this geographical area we do not consider, in this chapter, the funds owned by the Saudi Arabian Monetary Authority (SAMA) as a typically representative SWF, even though they are fairly large and have been classified as a SWF in the previous chapter. SAMA is actually the central bank of the Kingdom of Saudi Arabia, not a dedicated fund. This is so atypical that Saudi Arabia assumed the role of observer and not participant in the IMF's International Working Group which defined the Santiago Principles (see Chapter 7).

SWFs in the Middle East (Gulf Cooperation Countries (GCC) plus Iran) have assets ranging between US$980 billion and US$1,478 billion. In North Africa, the Libyan and Algerian funds have assets ranging between US$112 billion and US$117 billion. The total for the MENA region therefore comprises between US$1,092 and US$1,595 billion. Focusing on the Middle East and comparing with our previous years' estimates[51] ranging from US$1,156 billion to US$1,818 billion, the value of SWF assets in this region has decreased by an average of almost US$260 billion or 17%[52]. GCC countries suffered during the 2007-2009 crisis because of the fall in the price of oil, the tightening of international credit conditions, the collapse of the real estate market and the increased vulnerability of domestic banks. Middle Eastern SWFs were therefore called on to bail out their own domestic economies, diverting funds from foreign investment and instead directing them to domestic banks and equity markets. They were also called upon to meet fiscal deficits. With a feeble economic recovery, their SWF growth will essentially depend on the price of oil (see previous chapter).

For the Asian countries we have analysed the non-commodity SWFs of Singapore and China, which finance themselves with fiscal or balance-of-payments surpluses. Paradoxically we found that the most important SWFs in terms of assets on this continent are two extreme cases as far as country size is concerned.

Asian SWFs total an amount fluctuating between US$1,269 and US$1,342 billion. Compared with our previous year's estimate[53] of US$1,355 billion, the value of SWF assets in this region has decreased on average by US$50 billion or almost 4%. This appears to be a better performance than the GCC countries. However, the situations are quite different: while China gained 12%, reaching total assets of US$852 billion, Singaporean funds lost on average 28%, going down to a total ranging from between US$299 billion and US$367 billion. The pace of both Chinese and Singaporean fund activities slowed in the first quarter 2009 to reappear in the market again in the second half of the year, after having adapted their investment strategies to the new financial environment.

For European countries, the most significant SWFs in terms of size are the commodity funds of Norway and Russia. Here the situations are also quite different. While Norway's fund reached US$431 billion in September 2009, recording one of the best quarters ever, Russian funds went down to a combined amount of US$168 billion in December 2009 from US$225 billion the previous year (25% less), with the Reserve Fund risking disappearance by 2010.

In this chapter we provide a common structure for every SWF in order to analyse the following points:

- type, ownership, and size

- objectives and organisation

- portfolio characteristics and main shareholdings

- transparency

- other entities (i.e. entities belonging to the same government, definable as SWFs according to the classification provided in Chapter 2, but less representative in terms of history and size).

When there was insufficient direct information, we used various indirect sources[54]. For the section on transparency we have used Edwin Truman's Scoreboard for Sovereign Wealth Funds[55] and the Sovereign Wealth Fund Institute's website. While the information from these useful sources was thoroughly verified and compared, in some cases the results should still be treated with caution.

United Arab Emirates: ADIA and Dubai Inc

Type, ownership and size

The Abu Dhabi Investment Authority (ADIA) is owned by the government of Abu Dhabi, the largest and richest in terms of natural resources (it produces 90% of UAE's petroleum) of the seven emirates that make up the sovereign federal state of UAE. ADIA is the richest SWF on the planet, even though some recent estimates have reassessed this. They found that the value of its assets fluctuated between US$282 billion and US$627 billion at the end of 2008, instead of reaching US$800 billion, as many estimates reported previously. This wide margin of variation is due to this SWF's opacity: the fund has never publicly disclosed the value of its assets under management, and its investment activity is particularly difficult to track, adding to its air of secrecy.

However, it has been ascertained that the emirate's funds likely suffered significant losses because of the 2007-2009 financial crisis (the exact size of the loss can only be estimated). According to Setser and Ziemba[56], estimates circulating until 2009 hypothesising ADIA's assets at US$875 billion were overstated. Based on balance-of-payments data, the oil price and a plausible portfolio allocation, they estimated ADIA's value at closer to US$500 billion as of December 2007. They also calculated losses varying between US$140 billion and US$180 billion for 2008, equivalent to 28-36% of its portfolio value in December 2007, with the fund's value dropping to around US$328 billion in December 2008. Other analysts have also reassessed ADIA's value. The Institute of International Finance estimated ADIA's losses at around 25% of its value and that the fund was worth about US$282 billion in

December 2008[57]. The retrenchment of ADIA's assets has contributed to rendering the fund less frightening to Western recipients.

ADIA was established in 1976 to replace the Financial Investment Board, created in 1967 as part of Abu Dhabi's ministry of finance. The government exercises authority and supervision over this entity, although it is legally autonomous under a 1981 law that separates owners' and managements' roles and responsibilities.

The fund derives its financial resources from petroleum and specifically from the Abu Dhabi National Oil Company (ADNOC) and its subsidiaries which transfer a dividend to ADIA.

ADIA's operations are carried out by several SWEs. These include Tasameem and Tamweelview European Holdings in the real estate sector; Procific, an investment corporation located in the Cayman Islands; and Tannadice Investments.

In 2006 the government of Abu Dhabi established the Abu Dhabi Investment Council (ADIC) and transferred to the latter the domestic assets divested by ADIA. In this restructuring, ADIA received the mandate to manage foreign investments, while ADIC was put in charge of domestic ones. For this reason, we did not consider ADIC as a SWF in our classification in Chapter 2.

Objectives and organisation

According to official statements, ADIA's investment strategy is long-term, aimed at preserving and increasing financial wealth to ensure and maintain the emirate's future wellbeing.

The members of its board of directors, the supreme body controlling the authority, are all experienced public officials appointed by government decree. The board is chaired by Sheikh Khalifa bin Zayed Al Nahyan, president of the UAE. The board's task is to supervise and strategically direct the fund, but it does not get involved in operational decision-making. That is the job of the managing director responsible for the fund's management, as well its legal representative, who is completely independent from the government. The managing director is assisted by an investment committee and a number of advisory committees.

Portfolio and main shareholdings

ADIA invests in many different financial instruments: corporate shares quoted on the stock markets of industrialised and emerging markets, public and private bonds, local and regional real estate investments (funds or direct investments), and private equity funds.

ADIA's investment strategy has changed over the years. When first founded it tended to be cautious and conservative, trading mainly in liquid assets. It preserved its anonymity by acquiring small stakes, thus avoiding the obligation to disclose its participations in listed Western companies. In the last decade, however, the fund's investment activity has rapidly grown, with an increase in the number of publicly recorded transactions together with a rise in the level of risk. During the 2007-2009 crisis, the fund started to abandon its legendary opacity in favour of a more open and transparent approach. ADIA has consistently improved the volume and tone of its media coverage in the international business press in a strategy aimed at reassuring Western and domestic public opinion.

Although it is quite difficult to extrapolate ADIA's investment strategies and performance because of its limited transparency and scarce reporting (which we hope will be improved by the forthcoming official report for 2009 due to be published in spring 2010), it is still possible to gauge portfolio structure in geographic, currency and sectoral terms. Information that follows is thus largely based on various indirect sources; there are some cases in which interviews with ADIA's managing director are specifically cited.

Sheikh Ahmed Bin Zayed Al Nahyan, managing director of ADIA, reports[58] that portfolio allocation is as follows:

- between 40% and 60% to global equities

- between 15% and 30% to fixed income

- the remainder divided between other asset classes including real estate, private equity, alternative investments and infrastructure.

According to Rachel Ziemba's estimates[59], the remaining part can be broken down as follows:

- 5-10% in private equity

- 5-8% in real estate

- 5-10% in alternative investments.

Around 60% of ADIA's assets are invested in index-replicating strategies: S&P indices in the US and MSCI indices in the rest of the world for equities; for fixed income, various indices such as the Barclays Corporate Bond index, the JP Morgan Government Bond Index, as well as the Barclays Inflation Linked Bond index are used[60].

ADIA's portfolio is fairly well balanced geographically as well as sectorally, even though in 2007-2008 it placed a greater focus on the financial sector and particularly on private equity, where it invested no less than US$50 million per fund. Transactions in the financial sector accounted for 50% of the total value in the period 2000-2008, followed by energy and utilities with 39%.

From the geographical point of view, the fund allocates roughly 35-50% of its investments to the US, 25-35% to Europe, 10-20% to Asia and 15-25% to emerging markets[61].

The currency composition of its portfolio is estimated to be 45% in dollars, 40% in euros and pounds sterling, 10% in emerging market currencies and 5% in yen.

Most of the equity investments are in publicly-listed companies where ADIA typically owns less than 5%, since it is not interested in getting control of the companies it invests in. In this way it is not required to disclose investments to market supervisory authorities.

About 80% of its portfolio is invested by external asset managers.

According to some estimates[62], its portfolio made an annual average return of 10% until 2007, more than many other institutional investors. But this figure is not confirmed by official sources.

Some of its most notable shareholdings are in the financial sector:

- it holds convertible bonds in Citigroup, corresponding to 4.9% of its capital

- 9% of Apollo Management, a US private equity fund

- 20% of Ares Management, another US private equity fund

- 8% of Efg-Hermes, an Egyptian private equity fund

- 9.8% of Macquarie International Infrastructure Fund.

In addition it holds stakes in:

- AP Alternative Asset (40%)

- AIG Private Bank (100%)

- Tunisian Bank (40%)

- Arab Banking Corporation (28%)

- Arab International Bank (25%)

- HBOS, HSBC, Nordea Bank, Royal Bank of Scotland, Barclays, Aviva, and Lloyds.

In the telecoms sector it owns shares in Vodafone, British Telecom and Qatar Telecom; in IT, Taiwan Semiconductor and Mediatek; in the energy and raw materials sectors it has stakes in Anglo American, British Petroleum, Royal Dutch Shell, Rio Tinto, BHP Billiton and Cosmo Oil; in the pharmaceutical industry it holds shares in GlaxoSmithKline; in retail, in Tesco; in the food sector in Cadbury Schweppes and Diageo; in tobacco in Imperial Tobacco Group and British American Tobacco.

The fact that a large share of its portfolio is in stocks contributed to high yields in the three years from 2005 to 2007, and was a decisive factor in the fund's growth. However, these same investments, along with those in alternative instruments, generated significant losses over the last year, estimated by Setser and Ziemba at around US$140-180 billion in 2008. This effectively cancelled out most of the returns stemming from oil price rises.

Nevertheless, loss estimates cannot be considered completely reliable, given the fund's opacity, nor definitive if the fund holds on to its investments instead of realising losses. In any case the financial crisis was instructive: when financial income is correlated with global economic growth, as is the case for oil-exporting countries, profits should not be invested in businesses related to that growth. On the contrary, stabilisation funds as well as SWFs should follow the opposite logic.

Transparency

ADIA's is very low. In its 30 years of existence, the fund has never publicly declared the value of its portfolio nor has it disclosed a list of its shareholdings.

Truman's transparency classification puts ADIA in last place out of a total of 44 funds, with nine points out of 100. Even the Linaburg-Maduell index (see Chapter 5) assigns it a very low mark of three out of ten for 2009. This is all the more worrisome due to the fund's size. Its performance in terms of governance and reporting is particularly unsatisfactory. It must be recognised that the principles of transparency and accountability are not at the heart of the corporate universe in the GCC countries, and therefore it should not come as a surprise that GCC SWFs are particularly opaque.

This lack of transparency did not prevent a representative of ADIA being elected co-chair of the working group set up by the IMF to define the Santiago Principles. (Indeed perhaps it was the reason why their involvement was sought.) To adapt to the principles established among IMF members, ADIA promised greater transparency in revealing the investments in its portfolio.

Other entities

When considering the complex financial apparatus of the UAE, inextricable links between state finance and the royal family's wealth emerge. Personal wealth and public wealth are mixed up in a labyrinth of funds, companies, investment vehicles, state-owned enterprises, sovereign-wealth enterprises, subsidiaries and holdings. All of these are quite difficult to disentangle.

Starting with Abu Dhabi, in addition to ADIA we have identified the additional SWFs of the Mubadala Investment Company and the International Petroleum Investment Company (IPC). ADIC, established in 2006 to manage the emirate's domestic assets and focusing on internal development, has not been considered a SWF.

Mubadala[63], created in 2002, with assets of approximately US$22 billion at June 2009 and directly owned by the Abu Dhabi government, has the mandate of diversifying Abu Dhabi's investments and setting up strategic partnerships in high-tech sectors. It is involved in areas such as aerospace, energy, industry, healthcare, ICT and infrastructure, with the goal of developing the emirate's economy. The fund has also invested extensively in energy and utilities, particularly in renewable technologies as the energy mix worldwide moves away from hydrocarbons and Abu Dhabi focuses on becoming a global leader in sustainable energy technologies. Together with aerospace these sectors represent 50% of all deals made between 2000 and 2008[64], proving to be the most important sectors for the fund.

Mubadala is quite different to ADIA not only in terms of size, but also and especially in terms of transparency and style, presenting itself more as a private equity fund than a SWF. It is the most transparent fund in the region and among the most transparent in the world. The Linaburg-Maduell Transparency Index assigned it the maximum score of ten in the third-quarter 2009. It published its first annual report in 2008[65] and is continuing to publish six-monthly financial statements. Reports include detailed information – audited by international firms – on financial investments and results, something completely unknown to funds in this region. This clearly differentiates Mubadala from its larger, opaque competitor ADIA, as well as from the other funds in the Gulf.

In spite of its original focus on the domestic economy, Mubadala has also invested heavily abroad. Before 2008, 44% of Mubadala investments were in OECD countries and about 25% were in foreign emerging markets. Mubadala owns stakes in AMD (19%), Carlyle Group (7.5%), Ferrari (5%), Kor Hotel Group (50%), LeasePlan Corporation (25%), Libya Exploration (10%), Pearl Energy (100%),

Piaggio Aero Industries (32%), SR Technics (36%) and The John Buck Company (25%) to mention a few. However, in 2008 the fund refocused its attention on the development and diversification of Abu Dhabi's economy. This reconfirmed its central role and continued to differentiate it from ADIA. With the unfolding of the financial crisis of 2007-2009, the fund significantly contributed to the resilience of the emirate's economy through an increased emphasis on joint-venture deals, thus strengthening its role as an actively involved investor.

The International Petroleum Investment Company (IPIC) was established as a 50-50 venture between ADIA and ADNOC in 1984. It is now an independent company wholly owned by the government of Abu Dhabi and has assets of US$14 billion[66]. It is run by Sheikh Mansour bin Zayed Al Nahyan, the minister of presidential affairs and chairman of IPIC. IPIC is funded by petroleum revenues. Its investment strategy focuses on foreign investments in the energy and petrochemicals sector, in line with the emirate's goal of deepening its expertise in the oil industry and investing in downstream capacity. IPIC has partnerships with several leading companies all over the world. In March 2008 it acquired Aabar Investments, revealing a tendency towards diversifying its investments away from the energy sector. In fact, in the same year, through Aabar, IPIC bought stakes in the German carmaker Daimler (US$2.7 billion) and in the Italian bank UniCredit (US$63 million). As a SWF, IPIC resembles Mubadala with its focus on domestic economic transformation and sectoral diversification of the Emirates, as opposed to the focus of ADIA. However, in contrast to Mubadala and more in line with ADIA, IPIC is not a transparent fund; the Linaburg-Maduell transparency Index (LMTI) awarded it a score of three out of ten in 2009.

Dubai is another emirate of the UAE. In addition to being the least endowed with oil resources, it was hit the hardest by the global financial crisis due to its links with the global economy, its reliance on the real estate sector, a higher level of indebtedness and dependence on foreign capital, and its smaller oil-related fiscal revenues. The flight of foreign capital and the stock market crash in mid-2008 caused the investment bubble in the real estate sector to burst, leaving many state-owned corporations heavily indebted. The total debt of Dubai World, one of the investment vehicles in Dubai's universe, is estimated at US$80-100 billion, more than matching the emirate's 2008 GDP of US$82 billion.

This situation made intervention by the Dubai government unavoidable. A decision was made to reorganise the complex structure of Dubai's state-owned investment vehicles informally labelled as 'Dubai Inc' with the main purpose of restoring investor confidence and consolidating the debt burden. Following this restructuring, in 2009 Dubai's companies were organised into three groups: the Investment Corporation of Dubai (ICD), directly managed by the Government of Dubai; Dubai World, another holding company under the umbrella of Dubai's government and parent of Istithmar; and Dubai Holding, the ruler of Dubai, Sheikh Mohammed bin Rashid Al Maktoum's holding company for his personal assets.

In the classification provided in the previous chapter, we considered the Investment Corporation of Dubai and Istithmar as SWFs. We excluded Dubai Holding because it is funded by the personal wealth of Dubai's ruler and therefore behaves more like a private equity fund than a SWF.

The Investment Corporation of Dubai (ICD) was established in 2006 by transferring investments from the ministry of finance's portfolio in order to diversify Dubai's economy, thus reducing dependency on petroleum exports. ICD, with assets of between US$20 billion and US$82 billion according to the different estimates (the fund is rather opaque and its LMTI rating for 2009 is very low, four out of ten), gained more importance after the financial crisis, playing an important role in the reorganisation of the emirate's finances. Its most important holdings include the Dubai Stock Exchange (owning 20% of Nasdaq and 21% of the London Stock Exchange, which in turn owns the Italian Stock Exchange), Dubai Aluminium Company, Dubai World Trade Centre, Emirates Group, Emaar Properties, Emirates National Oil Company and several of Dubai's banks. Its foreign holdings include 3% in EADS, 2% of Sony, 6% of HSBC and 3% of Icici, the largest Indian bank.

Dubai World, which originally should have come under the umbrella of ICD, was finally granted the status of an independent holding company directly controlled by the government of Dubai. It is the most indebted of Dubai's investors, particularly because of the real estate investments of two of its controlled companies: Nakheel and Limitless. The former is the owner of the US$3.5 billion Sukuk bond issue that came to maturity on December 2009 and required debt restructuring, thus provoking a serious crisis of confidence among GCC investors. Its visionary real estate projects included Palm Jumeirah, the Waterfront, Palm Deira, etc. Limitless is another real estate developer with projects in many countries around the world. Dubai World is also owner of DP World, a profitable logistics company, one of the largest marine terminal operators in the world with 49 terminals across 31 countries as of March 2009.

Another entity belonging to Dubai World is Istithmar, the fund we classified as a SWF in Chapter 2. Istithmar was established in 2003 and owns US$9 billion in assets. It is an aggressive SWF with a diversified portfolio of private equity, hedge funds, venture capital, real estate and other alternative assets on a worldwide basis. It has participations, among others, in Barneys New York (90%), Cirque du Soleil (10%), Standard Chartered Bank (3%), and RMS Queen Elizabeth II (100%). In 2008, about three quarters of its investments were concentrated in the real estate sector, with important shareholdings in the US (Mandarin Oriental Hotels), the UK (Turnberry Golf Resort), and Sub-Saharan Africa (US$275 million in property resorts)[67]. The fund prefers minority stakes. In the period 2006-2008, Istithmar was an active, high-profile, aggressive investor, buying prestigious companies in the developed world, with high leverage. Following the financial crisis and the flight of capital from Dubai, this high leverage became a problem requiring the fund to divest some of its holdings such as Time Warner and Intercontinental. While it was quite highly leveraged in 2006, this significantly decreased in 2008[68]. Istithmar then rebalanced its portfolio away from real estate, although in 2009 this still made up about 60% of its total portfolio. The crisis reduced the value of its managed assets by US$1 billion in 2008, or 10% of its 2007 value. However, returns since its creation in 2003 remained high in 2010 at about 10%. Moreover, the fact that it was explicitly excluded by the Dubai government from the wider restructuring of Dubai World, meant it was considered financially sound.

Other participations by Dubai World include Economic Zones World (EZW), global provider of industrial and logistic solutions for economic zones and technology parks; Drydocks World, a leading company in ship repair, conversion, new building and other logistic activities for ports; Leisurecorp, with the aim of developing and managing golf initiatives and related real estate investments worldwide; and Dubai Natural Resources World, investing in energy resources and committed to making a positive contribution to sustainable development.

Dubai Holding, the third pillar in the restructured Dubai Inc, is the owner of Dubai International Capital, Dubai Group, Jumeirah Group, Tatweer, Dubai Properties and Sama Dubai among the others.

In addition to the two most well-known emirates in the UAE analysed so far, we still need to mention the country's smallest SWF, Rak Investment Authority belonging to the emirate of Ras al-Khaimah. Formed in 2005 and funded by the emirate's petroleum revenues, it is modestly sized at US$1.2 billion and invests mainly in the emirate's economy with the purpose of attracting investment to Ras al-Khaimah. Following the crisis it is plausible that it will concentrate on domestic investment, abandoning international economic expansion and trying to intercept investment flows taking flight from Dubai. Despite its domestic focus, it has extensive interests in Georgia and India. In Georgia, RAKIA established a Free Industrial Zone in 2008 to develop a world-class sea port at Poti. In India the fund is cooperating with the Andhra Pradesh Industrial Infrastructure Corporation to establish the Hyderabad Economic City. RAKIA has also recently signed an agreement with South Sumatra province in Indonesia to develop biotechnology parks.

To complete this outline of UAE's SWFs, we conclude with the Emirates Investment Authority (EIA), created in 2007 with the mandate to manage the UAE's sovereign wealth on a federal basis. This is the first SWF owned by all seven emirates of the federation. The financial crisis could have been an opportunity for EIA to assume a leading role in the reorganisation of the financial institutions of the country and to develop the UAE's SWFs in a strategic fashion, representing a unified investment front for the federation. However, this did not happen. The new strategic plan simply identified the key priority sectors for investment (telecommunications was identified as the priority for 2009). EIA has a series of stakes in companies in the Persian Gulf, including Etisalat, Gulf International Bank, United Arab Shipping Company, First Gulf

Bank and Gulf Investment Corporation, but also has the mandate to invest outside the region. As of 2010 it had not provided the value of its assets. The only available estimate is Monitor Group and Feems' report of between US$10 billion and US$20 billion.

Kuwait: KIA

Type, ownership, size

KIA (Kuwait Investment Authority), the investment authority of the government of Kuwait, manages two funds: the General Reserve Fund (GRF) and the Future Generations Fund (FGF). The first is the government's treasury entity and receives all state oil revenues, as well as owning the state's holdings (including shares in public corporations). The second was created in 1976 with the transfer of 50% of GRF's assets. It receives at least 10% of state oil revenues annually. KIA does not own any of the funds it manages as these are the property of the government of Kuwait.

KIA was established in steps, beginning in 1953 when the Kuwait Investment Board was founded with its head office initially in London. In 1965 the Kuwait Investment Board changed its name to Kuwait Investment Office (KIO). In 1982 KIA was founded to take control of all the Kuwaiti ministry of finance's activities, as well as to manage the two above-mentioned funds (GRF and FGF). KIA also became the holding company of KIO, which remained KIA's London branch and continues to help manage FGF's activities. In 1990 these entities ensured Kuwait's survival by supporting the government in exile at the time of the Iraqi invasion, as well as during the country's subsequent reconstruction.

In December 2008 KIA had assets in the region of US$169 billion to US$228 billion, according to various estimates. The lower figure came from Monitor Group[69]. They were reporting the declaration by KIA's managing director, in a closed session of the Kuwaiti parliament in February 2009, that assets had fallen to $169 billion at the end of 2008. The upper bound came from Setser and Ziemba's estimates[70].

The FGF, which invests mainly abroad in stocks and alternative instruments, represents about 80% of total assets, whereas the GRF has the remaining 20%.

Kuwait's SWEs include the National Technology Enterprises Company of Kuwait (NTEC), St Martins Property, Kuwait Real Estate Investment Consortium and the Kuwait China Investment Company (KCIC).

Objectives and organisation

The objective of KIA and its precursors, as enunciated by its founder (a ruling sheik) and a 1982 law, is to ensure real positive long-term returns, thus providing future generations with an alternative to finite oil reserves. This objective was elaborated as follows:

1. achieve a rate of investment return that exceeds market benchmarks on a three-year average

2. achieve a positive reputation on global financial markets

3. incentivise excellence in Kuwait's private sector not only by managing public shareholdings but also by financing various national entrepreneurial initiatives, and promoting the role of local financing companies and privatisation programs.

KIA is also dedicated to training Kuwaiti human capital, a crucial factor for the country's development.

KIA is an independent public authority managed by its board of directors, which defines investment strategies and is presided over by the ministry of finance. Four of its nine members are political, whereas at least three out of the other five must be non-political with experience in financial investing. The board elects a managing director who must not be from the political sphere.

Currently KIA's organisation reflects the industry's best practices based on a divisional structure. Following strategic consulting in 2006, separate divisions were established for traditional and non-traditional investing as well as direct shareholding in other public funds.

KIA has a specific code of conduct with a series of ethics rules its employees are obliged to follow.

Portfolio and main shareholdings

At one time strictly conservative and biased towards US debt securities, only recently has KIA's portfolio diversified into riskier investments. Historically it has been a conservative investor, searching for minority stakes and avoiding public disclosure of its investments. Most of the KIA portfolio, until 2004, was invested in US Treasuries, with only 2.5% in real estate, 1.5% in private equity funds, a few historical shareholdings in Daimler-Benz and BP purchased in the '70s and almost no exposure to emerging markets.

In 2004 Kia increased its stock holdings (setting a target of 60%), alternative instruments (private equity, hedge funds and derivatives) and its exposure to emerging markets, at the same time reducing US debt securities. The percentage of KIA's portfolio invested in hedge funds and private equity rose from 0% in 2003 to 15% in 2007. This change in strategy was due to the personality of Bader Al Sa'ad, appointed managing director in 2004. He revolutionised not only the organisation, but also KIA's investment strategy, modelling it on the base of Yale and Harvard University endowments, considered examples of institutional investors.

The allocation of KIA's stocks to various geographic regions depends on their economic weight in terms of global GDP. According to some estimates, at the end of 2007, KIA's portfolio was composed of 52% US stocks, 33% European stocks and 10% Asian stocks, in particular Japanese. In 2008 the US/EU percentage decreased to a combined 70% due to an increase in emerging market stocks, particularly from the Middle East and Asia, that doubled its quota according to a strategic decision taken in 2005.

KIA invests in equities (55-65% of asset allocation), bonds (8-12%), real estate (8-12%), alternative assets and hedge funds (3-7%).

From the sectoral point of view, KIA has recently preferred the financial sector, with the acquisition of shares in US, EU and Asian banks. In particular KIA bought stakes in troubled US banks (Citigroup and Merrill Lynch) despite the sharp fall in their shareholding prices. It was in every respect a bail out, justified by the fact that the authority saw this operation as a long-term investment. It thus spent a total of US$5 billion in January 2008 on these two US banks. Out of the total value of 2000-2008 deals (US$11 billion), the financial sector counted for 82%.

Around 50% of its portfolio is assigned to external fund managers. KIA is a discreet and passive investor, not aiming at companies' operational control.

All of its investments must be made without contracting debt, as KIA is barred from using leverage.

Some of its most important shareholdings such as Daimler and British Petroleum (BP) have been held since the 1970s and 1980s. It holds 7.2% of Daimler and 3.3% of BP. Other significant shareholdings in manufacturing include 8% of GEA Group (Germany), BAE Systems and Rolls-Royce in the aerospace industry, and GlaxoSmithKline and AstraZeneca in pharmaceuticals. In the financial sector KIA holds 6% of Citigroup's shares, 4.8% of Merrill Lynch, 4% of Visa Group, 54% of Arab Insurance Group, 16% of Kuwait's Gulf Bank, as well as shares in HSBC, Royal Bank of Scotland, Barclays, Aviva and Lloyds. It recently made a significant acquisition in the Industrial and Commercial Bank of China with 10% of its capital.

In the energy-mining sector it holds shares in Rio Tinto, Royal Dutch Shell, Anglo American, BHP Billiton and Jordan Phosphate Mines Company; in telecoms, Mobile Telecommunications Kuwait (25%) and British Telecom; in the food sector it holds stakes in Cadbury Schweppes, Tesco and Unilever; and in the consumer goods sector it holds 24% of Victoria-Jungfrau Collection (Switzerland).

Like other SWFs, KIA was hard hit by the international financial crisis and there has been strong internal pressure to quantify losses. In fact KIA invested billions of dollars, over the last two years, in troubled Western banks, thus neutralising its windfall of oil revenues. Whereas average annual returns were well over 10% in previous years, in 2008 estimated losses reduced its asset value by about US$40 billion or 20%.

To add to the collapse of results was the slump in the local stock market due to the weakening of investors' confidence and the plunge in the oil price, with the Kuwait Stock Exchange losing 40% in less than one year. Local media attributed the responsibility to KIA for dissipating national wealth. As a result there were strong domestic pressures in Kuwait (and other Middle Eastern countries) to redirect SWF investments to domestic economies. Thus KIA had to intervene in the Kuwaiti Stock Market, establishing a multi billion dollar fund for rescuing Kuwaiti companies and purchasing 24% shares of Kuwait Gulf Bank, one of the largest in the country. This strong political interference was not usual in Kuwait, even if the authority had to regularly report in Parliament about its investment activity. The government's approval of a stimulus bill and the issuing of US$1.3 billion in treasury bonds are expected to ease political pressure.

At the beginning of 2009, the fund seemed more involved in supporting Kuwaiti companies and stock markets than investing abroad, decreasing the ratio of international shares on the total of managed assets. This does not mean, however, that the authority halted international investment. A few transactions were recorded in international markets at the beginning of 2009. Nevertheless, the crisis left its mark on KIA in the form of a financial shift of power in the relations between parliament and the authority, with KIA now subject to requests of more accountability and greater political control over its investment strategy. As normally happens in periods of crisis, technocrats yielded ground in favour of politicians. However, it is still not clear whether this will result in a more conservative strategy by KIA, in an increased focus on the domestic economy or, simply, greater transparency.

Transparency

Truman's scoreboard assigns KIA 48 points out of 100, putting it in the middle of the ranking. Its weakest areas are reporting and defining the portfolio's code of conduct. KIA's financial statements are certified by an external accounting firm. The Linaburg-Maduell Index assigned KIA a score of six out of ten in third-quarter 2009, i.e. intermediate but not sufficient.

Kuwait's Law 47 of 1982 states that KIA must present a detailed annual report of its investment activity to the council of ministers and parliament. However, providing information to the public is punishable by law. It's hard, therefore, to hold up KIA as a good example of transparency. Nevertheless it remains the only Middle Eastern SWF accountable to a parliament that has the authority to criticise and scrutinise it, as events have demonstrated.

Libya: LIA

Type, ownership, size

LIA (Libyan Investment Authority) was established in 2006 by consolidating several pre-existing funds, including the Libyan Arab Foreign Investment Company (LAFICO) and the Oilinvest Company. LIA is thus a holding company with shares in government investment funds. This SWF, with estimated assets in the range of US$65-70 billion, is a commodity fund fed by oil and gas revenues.

LIA relies on the following SWEs: Libyan Arab Foreign Investment Company (LAFICO), the Economic and Social Development Fund of Libya (ESDF); Oilinvest; the Libyan Arab African Investment Company (LAAICO) and the Libyan African Investment Portfolio (LAP).

LAFICO, founded in 1981, is the oldest investment entity in Libya. Its mandate is to invest both domestically and abroad in diversified sectors. ESDF, established in February 2006, invests domestically across a number of sectors to promote Libya's development and support its poor. Oilinvest, founded in 1988, invests in the oil sector in Africa and Europe. LAAICO invests in Africa in more than 25 countries and in diversified sectors in order to support the continent's economic development, to promote free trade across Africa and to facilitate the absorption of technology by African firms. LAP, established in 2006 by the Libyan Government, is endowed with US$8 billion in capital and invests primarily in Africa in diversified sectors.

Objectives and organisation

LIA has the mandate to invest its funds domestically and abroad so as to create a balanced portfolio composed of high-value investments, diversifying the Libyan economy and reducing its dependence on energy resources.

LIA is run by a board of directors composed of seven members who exercise decision-making power; some are prominent politicians whereas others are important bankers. In addition, the board consults with a committee of international financial experts. The current managing director is a former governor of the central bank.

Portfolio and main shareholdings

Investments follow commercial criteria based on financial yield considerations. Most of the funds are managed by Western banks and financial institutions.

Very little information is available on this SWF's shareholdings and portfolio structure.

In terms of sectors, 53% of the total value (US$5.3 billion) of deals reported in the period 2000-2008 was concentrated in real estate, while 36% was directed to the financial sector. Other sectors have much more limited shares.

In terms of geographical destination, LAFICO has a significant interest in Italian companies. In fact LIA and its predecessor have a long history of investing in Italy, starting with the controversial entry of Libya into Fiat in 1977 with 15% of ordinary share capital. This share was sold in 1986. The history of Libyan investment in Italy intensified in the year 2000 when LAFICO returned to buy 2% of Fiat and 3% of Capitalia, which subsequently became 5%. Its presence in the Italian banking sector, diluted due to the Capitalia-UniCredit merger, was reinforced in the autumn of 2008 with the acquisition of 4.23% of UniCredit for over €1 billion. This share then grew to 4.99% with the subscription of convertible loan stock of €550 million. LAFICO also owns shares in Juventus (7.8%), Finpart (9%) and Olcese (31%), all of them Italian companies. Other participations are in Dar Hotels and Resorts in Tunisia (53%), Le Méridien Amman in Jordan (50%), Corinthia Group (50%) in Malta, Circle Oil (30%) in Ireland and the Housing Bank of Algeria (15%).

In 2007 LIA also established a joint investment with the Qatari fund for US$2 billion.

Transparency

The level of this SWF's transparency is not high. Data on investments are given only through the press and media, and there is no periodic reporting to inform stakeholders.

Since LIA is not included in Truman's scoreboard we refer to the Linaburg-Maduell Index (see Chapter 5) for transparency, which gives a very low rating of two out of ten in third-quarter 2009.

For the future, however, LIA, which also participated in the IMF's International Working Group, stated its commitment to adhere to higher transparency standards. This was reflected in a decree issued by the Libyan government in 2008 requiring LIA to publish annual reports of its investment activity in English and Arabic on its website. However, it is not clear whether this decree was followed up; at the end of 2009, it was still rather difficult to find information about LIA.

Singapore: Temasek Holdings and GIC

The case of the city-state of Singapore is one of the most significant due to the fact that its SWFs are a vital part of the government, not only in terms of economic strategy. Singapore's SWFs are Temasek Holdings and Government Investment Corporation (GIC), both state-owned.

To understand their characteristics, it is first of all necessary to clarify their role in Singapore's economic development. For more than three decades this city-state has been a significant outward foreign direct investor (FDI) and is one of the main international investors in emerging markets. From the geo-sectoral point of view, this FDI was aimed at overcoming the boundaries of small domestic markets characterised by limited potential growth in demand, investment and advanced technology.

From the institutional point of view, Singapore can count on large state-owned companies with a state-market relationship emphasising the role of the state more than the market (if compared to major developed economies). The Government Linked Companies (GLC), held directly by the ministry of finance as a stakeholder, supported domestic industrialisation in the 1960s and 1970s and in the following decades promoted internationalisation.

Temasek and GIC have made Singapore into one of the few examples in the world of a small country with no natural resources which accumulated an impressive amount of wealth then managed it rationally and professionally, thus allowing the nation to assume an important role on the global financial scene.

Let us now separately examine the two SWFs, beginning with Temasek, which launched Singapore's economic-financial strategy as a city-state "founded" on SWFs[71].

Type, ownership and size

In 1974 Temasek Holdings was created with the purpose of managing shareholdings in the GLCs and investing fiscal and external surpluses of various origins and types as well as income from shareholdings, domestically and abroad. Its shares are wholly owned by the ministry of finance. Temasek is not considered a SWF by the Singapore government, although it is considered such by the main international classifications. In July 2009 its assets were US$119 billion.

It is supported by four SWEs: Orchard Energy, Fullerton Financial Holdings, Fullerton Management and Aspen Holdings.

Objectives and organisation

Its goal is to professionally manage Singapore's state holdings in order to maximise their value for shareholders over the long term. Unlike GIC, Temasek is not only in charge of managing a financial portfolio, but is also in charge of managing state-owned enterprises in strategic sectors for the economic development of the city-state.

While wholly state-owned, Temasek is managed independently by an autonomous board whose members are drawn partly from politics and mostly from the private sector. The CEO Ho Ching – the Prime Minister's wife, and daughter-in-law of modern Singapore's first prime minister Lee Kuan Yew – was replaced in 2009 by Chip Goodyear, former CEO of BHP Billiton.

Portfolio and main shareholdings

Temasek holds shares (normally over 20% of share capital, and in many cases 50% or even 100%) in Singapore's largest corporations and thus has enormous influence over the city-state's economy. The fund also has significant stakes in foreign companies both directly and indirectly through its GLCs.

Its investment strategy is characterised by a large share of domestic investments, a long-term horizon, attention to corporate governance and an active shareholder approach.

Geographically speaking, 31% of Temasek's investments were located in Singapore as of March 2009, 27% in northern Asian countries (China, Taiwan and Korea) and 22% in OECD countries. This is followed by ASEAN (Association of South East Asian Nations, which has ten member countries including the Philippines, Indonesia, Malaysia, Singapore and Thailand) with 9%, southern Asia (India and Pakistan) with 7% and Latin America and others with 4%. The lion's share in this portfolio is represented by Asia, considered the most promising and profitable region, with a combined quota of 43% of the total. In 2008 the fund achieved its goal of reducing investments in domestic companies to no more than one-third of its portfolio and increasing international investments in Asia and OECD countries.

From the sectoral point of view, Temasek's portfolio covers the following sectors as of March 2009:

- banking and financial services (33%)

- telecoms and media (26%)

- transport and logistics (13%)

- real estate (9%)

- infrastructure, industrial engineering (6%)

- energy and natural resources (5%)

- high technology (1%)

- life sciences and healthcare, education and consumer goods (1%).

Recently most investments focused on the financial sector, reaching 33% of the total in March 2009. Some of the fund's most significant shareholdings in the banking-finance sector are:

- 74% of NIB Bank, one of Pakistan's most important banks

- 68% of Bank Danamon, one of Indonesia's most important banks

- 28% of DBS, an Asian group specialising in financial services

- 19% of Standard Chartered Bank

- 10% of the Hana Financial Group, a shareholding under scrutiny by the Korean government

- 8% of ICICI Bank, the largest private bank and principal provider of consumer credit in India

- 6% of China Construction Bank and 4% of the Bank of China, two of the four largest Chinese state banks.

In sum, as of March 2009 Temasek had holdings in seven important Asian banks and one significant Western bank. However, due to the financial crisis and losses registered by these holdings, it is unlikely that the fund's already large portfolio share in this sector will continue to increase. On the contrary, some shareholdings were sold last year such as the 9% in UBS, 4.5% in Citigroup, 14% in Merril Lynch, and 3% in Barclays.

The second most important sector for Temasek is telecommunications and media, which represent 26% of its total portfolio. The most important shareholdings in this sector include:

- 100% of MediaCorp, Singapore's main television broadcaster as well as its most important media group

- 100% of Singapore Technologies Telemedia, an information technology and telecoms company

- 54% of Singapore Telecommunications, a telecommunications giant based in Singapore with activities and investments in 20 Asian countries

- 42% of Shin Corporation, Thailand's primary telecom company, the acquisition of which generated substantial problems for Temasek and the government of Singapore

- 5% in Bharti Airtel, an Indian integrated telecom service provider.

Another strategically important sector is transport and logistics, which makes up 13% of Temasek's investments. Its strategic goal is to make the country into a global hub for energy transport and logistics. To that end it holds the following shares:

- 100% of PSA, a global port logistics giant based in Singapore

- 66% of Neptune Orient Lines, a globally integrated logistics company based in Singapore and known in Europe for its attempt to acquire Hapag-Lloyd, the Hamburg-based logistics company in the summer of 2008 (the operation was not concluded due to the strong reaction in Germany and intervention by the German government)

- 55% of Singapore Airlines, flagship airline of the city-state and logistics provider of airline services

- and 54% of SMRT, a leading Singapore multimodal logistics and transportation engineering company.

Another notable sector in which Temasek has invested is real estate, comprising 9% of total investments, with shareholdings in Mapletree Investments and Capital Land, both in Singapore.

The infrastructure and industrial engineering sectors make up 6% of total investments and also include some important shareholdings such as Singapore Technologies Engineering, SembCorp Industries and the Keppel Corporation.

The energy sector makes up 5% of Temasek's investments. The notable increase in raw materials prices in 2008 caused a strong revaluation of these shareholdings. This was behind the decision to slow down further acquisitions and monetise the existing ones, which led to the conversion into cash in September-October 2008 of Senoko Power and

PowerSeraya, whereas Temasek retained ownership of Singapore Power.

Just 1% of Temasek's investments are in the advanced technology sector but given its strong growth potential, this share is likely to increase. The same goes for healthcare and consumer goods sectors, which take up 1% of the portfolio.

Temasek holds shares in many important national companies in strategic sectors for the domestic economy, controlling six out of the 15 largest Singaporean companies, whose combined value represents 25% of the total Singapore stock exchange[72].

The value of the fund's assets dropped from US$134 billion in March 2008 to US$93 billion in March 2009. In July 2009 the value of the fund increased again to US$119 billion, representing 89% of its March 2008 value. On a year-on-year basis the fund lost 30% of the value of its assets, while compared to July 2009, after international stock markets recovered, the loss was reduced to 11%. Considering that its initial capitalisation was US$134 million, granted by the Singapore government, the fund's increase remains enormous and is due both to returns on investment and liquidity injections by the government, which were especially frequent during the 1990s. The declared rate of return in March 2009 was 16% on an annual basis from the start-up year, 1974. This rate was two points down on the return declared on March 2008 (18%). The total shareholder return on a one-year basis was -18% in March 2009. Negative returns recorded in 2008 were also due to some divestments in Western financial banks, which materialised losses that could have remained only hypothetical. Total net divestments in the year amounted to US$7 billion. The fund's creditworthiness and profitability have been confirmed by Standard & Poor's (AAA) and Moody's (AAA) ratings. This is one of the few Asian corporations outside Japan to receive such an excellent rating.

Some foreign investments have generated hostility, given the public nature of the fund. According to some commentators, Temasek has sometimes shown little sensitivity and insufficient knowledge of the political context of countries it has invested in (emblematic is the case of the Thailand Shin Corporation, which in addition to generating a loss of approximately US$2 billion caused a significant negative political reaction in Thailand).

Transparency

Truman's scoreboard assigns Temasek a rating of 45 out of 100, an intermediate position with low performance in terms of the explicitness of its investment strategies, but fairly positive in terms of reporting and auditing. The Linaburg-Maduell Index gives it the maximum rating of ten in third-quarter 2009. In fact Temasek publishes a detailed memorandum on its financial performance, investments, governance structure, and risk management strategies in its annual report, which has been available to the public on its website since 2004. In addition Temasek is required to provide detailed information on its portfolio, previously revised periodically (annually and quarterly), to the ministry of finance.

Finally, as a member of the IMF's International Working Group, its commitment to transparency is bound to increase.

* * *

The second pillar of Singapore's strategy as a city-state founded on SWFs is the GIC fund, which we will examine now.

Type, ownership and size

GIC is a global investment entity established in 1981 by the government of Singapore to manage currency reserves accumulated through balance- of-payments and other fiscal surpluses and to profitably invest excess national savings.

There are three sources of funds invested by GIC[73]:

1. budget surpluses (between 2000 and 2006 Singapore accumulated an annual average of US$5.5 billion in budget surpluses, equivalent to 5% of GDP)

2. currency exchange reserves exceeding the needs of monetary policy as managed by the Monetary Authority of Singapore (MAS)

3. surpluses coming from the Central Social Security Fund maintained through mandatory social contributions paid by Singapore workers.

GIC is wholly owned by the government of Singapore. It has investments in approximately 40 countries in over 2000 companies for estimated total assets fluctuating between US$180 billion and US$248 billion, making it one of the largest SWFs in the world.

GIC uses three SWEs for its operations:

1. GIC Asset Management invests in stocks, fixed income and foreign currency, with the goal of exceeding yields of certain market indices

2. GIC Real Estate, one of the ten largest real estate investors in the world, with over 200 investments in 30 countries

3. GIC Special Investments, specialised in venture capital investments, leveraged buyouts and various types of direct investments in companies; one of the largest private equity funds in the world.

Objectives and organisation

GIC's mission is to manage the currency reserves of the city-state of Singapore, preserving and increasing the purchasing power of these reserves for times of crisis; to contribute to the needs of the public budget; and to safeguard wealth for future generations. Over the medium term the goal is to exceed the returns of certain market indices. Its goals are thus exclusively financial.

The ministry of finance determines investment goals, time frames, risk parameters, and guidelines for managing the portfolio, but it does not interfere in operational investment decisions. The board of directors' task is to define policies for allocating investments and monitoring portfolio performance. It comprises both executive and non-executive members, split between three government members, four independents and six GIC executives. Management is responsible for investment transactions and is fully autonomous in carrying out the investment strategies defined by the board, with a complete separation between ownership and management.

The GIC puts a certain emphasis on risk management strategies as well as the importance of strong governance founded on persons of unquestionable integrity. Three committees have the task of ensuring that the fund acts according to ethical and fiscal norms.

GIC's organisational structure formally contains many of the features of the best Anglo-Saxon financial institutions, as pointed out by Clark and Monk[74], and can claim to be recognised by the international financial community as one of the best-managed SWFs worldwide.

GIC has the role of insurer of last resort, conceived to preserve Singapore's independence in case of financial international turmoil and to guarantee resources for long-term growth even in troubled circumstances. This was the original intention of its founding father, Prime Minister Lee Kuan Yew, when the fund was established in 1981 in a time of turbulent international financial markets. The main purpose was to protect the value of Singapore's savings and to earn a fair return on capital with them, not to maximise financial returns. This approach can be better understood if we look back at the Asian financial crisis of the late 1990s when those countries not endowed with sufficient reserves de facto gave up their sovereignty in exchange for the IMF's financial support, entailing the acceptance of its neo-liberal agenda. At that time Singapore already had sufficient resources, including GIC's assets, and was able to preserve its autonomy. This was certainly a lesson for all the economies in the region and reinforced Singapore's awareness of the importance of relying on its own resources in case of financial uncertainty. In order to guarantee the role of insurer of last resort, Singapore's constitution protects GIC's reserves from immediate political claims, with a mechanism that requires parliament's and the president's joint approval before tapping reserves. It is on this role of insurer of last resort, enshrined in the constitution, that GIC's political legitimacy is founded.

Portfolio and main shareholdings

GIC's portfolio is differentiated in terms of financial instruments and includes equities, fixed income, foreign exchange, commodities, money markets, alternative investments, real estate and private equity.

The geographical distribution of its portfolio[75], covering 40 countries, is structured as follows (as of 31 March 2009): 45% in America, mainly in the US (38%); 29% in Europe with 6% in the UK; 24% in Asia with 11% in Japan and 10% in North Asia; and 2% in Oceania. Most of the portfolio is therefore directed towards developed economies, even though in the last ten years there has been an increasing trend towards investing in emerging markets, particularly in Asia.

Its investments are broken down by type as follows[76]:

- 38% in public debt securities (28% in developed countries)
- 24% in fixed income securities
- 12% in real estate
- 11% in private equity, venture capital and infrastructure
- 7% in other types of alternative investments, including natural resources
- the remaining 8% is held in liquid assets.

This structure evolved over the years and it is interesting to note that recently more space has been given to emerging market government securities and shares, real estate, private equity and hedge funds.

Following is a list of the more significant shareholdings in the most important sectors. Holdings in private equity and venture capital funds in Asia, America, and Europe include Texas Pacific, Carlyle, Blackstone, Bain Capital, Providence, Permira, and Sequoia Capital, just to mention a few.

Shareholdings in quoted shares include:

- in the financial sector, Standard Chartered, China Construction Bank, DBS Group, Bank of China, Merrill Lynch, Barclays, Royal Bank of Scotland, China International Capital Corporation, Infrastructure Development Finance Company, and UBS

- in telecoms, Singapore Telecommunications, MobileOne, and Vodafone

- in logistics and transport, British Airports Authority, Associate British Ports Holdings, SembCorp Marine, Neptune Orient Lines, Singapore Airlines, Singapore

Airport Terminal Services, Beijing Capital International Airport, SMRT, China Cosco Holdings, and Air China

- in the industrial sector, Singapore Technologies Engineering, Keppel, SembCorp Industries, Citic, Rolls-Royce, Sinopec Shanghai Petrochemical, and AstraZeneca

- in the energy/mining sector, Singapore Petroleum, BP, Royal Dutch Shell, Rio Tinto, Anglo American, and BHP Billiton

- in the electronics sector, Chartered Semiconductor, Taiwan Semiconductor Manufacturing, Hon Hai Precision Industries, Infosys Technologies, High Tech Computer (HTC), MediaTek, and Siliconware Precision Industries

- in real estate, Mapletree Logistics, CapitaRetail China, CapitaMall Trust Management, Beijing Capital Land, Brixton, Dev Property, CapitaLand, British Land, Liberty International, and Great Portland Estates

- in the food sector, Singapore Food Industries, Unilever, Cadbury Schweppes; and in retail, Tesco, Sainsbury and Marks & Spencer Group.

Its holdings are impressive. The most important sectors are transport and logistics, energy and financial services.

As a consequence of the 2007-2009 financial crisis, GIC suffered a loss of more than 20% of its portfolio value on a yearly basis as of March 2009. In terms of profitability, the 20-year nominal annual rate of return in Singapore dollar terms fell from 5.8% in 2008 to 4.4% in 2009. It was 8.2% until 2006. In real terms, netting for global inflation, the rate of return fell from 4.5% in 2008 to 2.6% in 2009. From March 2009, however, global stock markets recovered strongly. GIC's portfolio therefore offset more than half of the previous year's losses.

Some of GIC's operations have drawn particular attention from the media, especially its investment of a total of US$20 billion in UBS and Citigroup in early 2008 in the wake of the financial crisis. As the crisis unfolded these banks suffered significant losses, which were reflected in their share. GIC converted its preferred stock holdings of 4% of Citigroup at a conversion price of US$3.25 a share, enabling the fund to recover its initial loss on the investment. UBS 9% shares, on the other hand, will take longer to recover. However, they have been kept in the portfolio with a long-term horizon, maintaining confidence that both banks will return to profitability.

Finally, it must be noted that the government tapped GIC's reserves for the first time during the recent crisis.

If we consider that GIC has preserved the value of Singapore savings in spite of the Asian crisis of 1997 and the dotcom bubble of 2000-2002 and that it is now recovering from the 2007-2008 financial crisis, it appears that the fund has succeeded in safeguarding the value of national savings and preserving financial stability, delivering on its promise of conserving political autonomy and enhancing economic security.

Transparency

Truman's scoreboard gives GIC 41 points out of 100, an intermediate rating slightly below that of Temasek. Its weakest area is defining portfolio behaviours.

According to the Linaburg-Maduell Index its level of transparency was six out of ten in third-quarter 2009.

GIC is required to report its activities to the ministry of finance on a monthly and quarterly basis, providing detailed information on performance, risks and portfolio allocation. Once a year its management meets the prime minister to discuss the previous year's situation regarding risk and performance. Financial information is audited on a yearly basis. Nevertheless it is not required to report to parliament and the fund has never disclosed the total value of its assets.

After the issuing of the Santiago Principles, which GIC adheres to as a member of the IWG, the fund has acknowledged the importance of improving transparency and has published on its website a financial report for the year 2008-09, including information on the geographic allocation of the portfolio, the asset mix and returns on investment. However, the report is still missing some fundamental information such as the value of the fund's total assets, and it is not as detailed and transparent as Temasek's.

China: CIC and Other Entities

The case of China is strategically and geopolitically important not only due to the size of its SWFs (a combined total of US$852 billion in assets), but more importantly because it is an expression of a global economic power. For this reason we will give ample space to CIC and the other Chinese SWFs. We will refer to direct[77] and indirect sources[78] as well as the international press.

Type, ownership and size

China established the China Investment Corporation (CIC) in September 2007 with an initial endowment of US$200 billion. Today the fund has US$298 billion in total assets. Given the fund's size and China's role as an emerging global superpower, the founding of CIC immediately drew the attention of financial markets and policymakers from many countries, especially the United States.

The creation of this SWF was the result of a two-year debate in the country regarding the use of the enormous and growing foreign currency reserves accumulated in the last decade at a monthly growth rate ranging from 2 to 4%. In December 2007 these reserves amounted to US$1,528 billion, in December 2008 they totalled US$1,946 billion, and in December 2009 they stood at US$2,399 billion[79]. They were accumulated as a result of current account surpluses starting at the end of the 1990s.

China has always invested the bulk of its excess reserves in US treasury bonds, characterised by low risk but also low returns. Between 2003 and 2006 yields from these bonds were estimated at between 2 and 4%, a modest return for an economy growing at an average annual rate of 10%. China's objective of keeping the renminbi (RMB) linked to the dollar created a monetary-currency mechanism that was formidably expensive in both economic and political terms. The debate between the ministry of finance (MOF) and the central bank (People's Bank of China or PBoC) sharpened due to the inability to better utilise the country's currency reserves. Various solutions were proposed to better use this wealth and the government finally opted for the proposal by the MOF to establish a SWF, announced in March 2007, with the goal of investing surplus currency revenues directly abroad. Strong resistance by the PBoC did not succeed in blocking the project, but translated into the onerous conditions defined by the state council for financing the CIC.

In September 2007 when the CIC was created, the ministry of finance issued 1,550 billion RMB (corresponding to US$200 billion) of debt in Chinese treasury bonds (with maturity of 10-15 years and return rates ranging between 4.3% and 4.45%) which it conferred to the CIC. This debt was then used by the CIC to acquire foreign currency from the PBoC. The CIC has to pay dividends to the MOF to cover financing costs. In this way, market risk is totally transferred to CIC, while currency risk is sustained by the MOF. The PBoC, on the other hand, is not subject to any risk.

The CIC is wholly owned by the Chinese government and reports directly to the state council, the country's highest executive and administrative body, and to the premier. This arrangement appears to have been conceived to solve the conflict between the PBoC and the ministry of finance regarding which authority had the mandate to manage the new fund.

According to *The Economic Observer*[80], CIC reached an agreement with the MOF in the summer of 2009 to consider the initial US$200 billion endowment as assets rather than debt. This will ease the pressure on the CIC, which has to pay the MOF roughly US$10 billion in interest every year to repay its initial debt. The agreement could entail CIC paying dividends to the MOF on a yearly basis.

CIC uses several SWEs. They include:

- the Central Huijin Investment Company (CHIC), established in 2003, which deals with domestic investment, particularly in the banking sector

- China Jianyin Investment, wholly owned by CHIC, which also deals with domestic investment, in particular debt restructuring

- the Stable Investment Corporation, which invests in short-term instruments, especially money market funds

- Beijing Wonderful Investments, which has direct shareholdings in foreign companies

- Fullbloom Investment Corporation

- Country Forest Limited

- Chengdong Investment Corporation.

Objectives and organisation

CIC's stated objectives are first to maximise long-term returns on investments using a well-balanced portfolio of foreign equities, and secondly to recapitalise state-owned domestic financial institutions by helping to enhancing their value.

Although the CIC is ultimately answerable to the state council, the composition of its board of directors makes it clear that the CIC is an emanation of the ministry of finance and is more under the influence of this body than that of the PBoC. The president is Lou Jiwei, ex-minister of finance and ex-vice-secretary general of the state council, a high-profile figure. The director general, Gao Xiqing, is also a key figure in the world of Chinese finance, having set up the Chinese stock exchange and the stock exchange supervisory committee and having been vice president of the national pension fund. The Board of Directors, with 11 members, is composed of political figures from the ministries involved in CIC as well as from the PBoC, but is more biased, in terms of composition, towards the MOF than the PBoC. It also includes independent members. The board must be approved by the state council. The management team, on the other hand, is composed mainly of technocrats with proven experience in managing public and private investments. The board of directors defines strategies and guidelines for investing, which the management team then implements, keeping its operational independence. In addition to these organs there are a board of supervisors and several committees.

Regarding surveillance, CIC is not subject to any regulatory authority since it answers directly to the state council and is on the same level as the PBoC and the other organs of financial oversight.

Portfolio and main shareholdings

The above described genesis has influenced CIC's investment strategies and targets. Being debt-based, CIC must respond to severe constraints in terms of the type of investments it can undertake. In fact the cost of borrowing from MOF, together with the expected appreciation of RMB, represent the minimum rate of return the fund must exceed in order to be economically sustainable in the long run. Considering that the cost of debt is roughly 4% and assuming an annual appreciation of the RMB of another 2%, the CIC must be able to deliver at least a 6% return just to break even. In the new financial scenario, this target appears not easy to achieve especially for those funds that can not count on a long history of investments and satisfying returns.

Its domestic shareholdings (with a counter-value of US$110 billion) included the immediate acquisition of Central Huijin Investment Company (CHIC), established in 2003, for US$67 billion, which meant taking over all of CHIC's shareholdings including 68% of the Bank of China, 35% of the Industrial and Commercial Bank of China, 48% of China Construction Bank, and 71% of China Everbright Bank. Shares of 50% of the Agricultural Bank of China and the China Development Bank (49%) were bought directly by the CIC for another US$40 billion.

CIC actually owns a large part of the Chinese banking and finance system, which represented 58% of all bank assets and 59% of all loans at the end of 2007.

Its first acquisitions abroad (where the remaining US$90 billion have been allocated) included US$3 billion for a 9.4% share in the Blackstone Group private equity fund, and US$5 billion for a 9.9% share of Morgan Stanley. The participation in the Blackstone Group dates back to before CIC was created, when the China Jianyin Investment Company, wholly owned by CHIC, stipulated an agreement with Blackstone.

Subsequent activity has preferred the acquisition of internationally recognised investment firms and private equity, consistent with the approach of using external managers and taking an indirect role in share investments. The external funds the CIC invested in between 2007 and 2008 include the JC Flower Fund for US$3 billion, the Reserve

Primary Fund for US$5.4 billion, JP Morgan Prime Money Market Fund for US$2.3 billion, Invesco AIM Liquid Assets Portfolio for US$2.1 billion and DWS Money Market Trust for US$1.5 billion.

This first wave of investments was flawed by an excessive geographical and sectoral concentration that caused several problems, especially with the unfolding of the financial crisis. While for Morgan Stanley the instrument of convertible stock consented to limit losses, in the case of Blackstone share prices plunged from US$31 in June 2007 to US$4.5 in January 2009, with a potential loss of 85% of the investment value. Not to mention the foreclosure of the Reserve Primary Fund that has generated fears of further losses in spite of CIC's reassuring declarations. The accumulation of all those losses has damaged CIC's reputation and roused domestic criticism about CIC's ability to invest in international markets.

However, at the end of 2008 CIC reported a net income of US$23 billion and total assets of US$298 billion. The return on its global portfolio for 2008 was -2.1%, while on the initial capital it was positive and equal to 6.8%, results that can be considered almost a success if taking into account the performance of other financial operators in international markets in the same year.

Investment activity slowed between end-2008 and 2009 for two main reasons. Firstly, the Chinese government's decision to deploy financial resources internally (the government itself undertook drastic fiscal measures in the form of a US$600 billion stimulus package). Secondly, CIC needed to rethink its investment strategy, redirecting its huge resources to diversified markets (emerging economies) and sectors (energy, commodities and the environment). After a period of standstill, CIC has undertaken a significant reorganisation, recruiting new talents and defining a new structure in order to implement the new strategy. In the second quarter of 2009 the fund started to invest again. The fund's investments in 2009 reached US$17.5 billion, with US$6 billion going into energy and natural resources in the second and third quarters[81]. In those sectors CIC acquired 11% of KazMunaiGas Exploration Production, a Kazakhstan based state-run energy company, for US$939 million; 45% of Nobel Oil Group based in Russia for US$300 million; 15% of the power plant developer AES Corporation for US$1.58

billion; 17% of Teck Resources Limited, a Canadian mining company; stakes in the Noble Group, specialised in supply chain management of commodities, particularly agricultural products; and in China, the Longyuan Power Group, a Chinese wind power generator. Since the second half of 2009 the fund has also targeted the hedge fund sector and real estate with investments of respectively US$2.7 billion and almost US$1 billion.

Expectations for 2009 were positive. CIC could earn more than 10% from its 2009 investments, following the financial markets' renaissance and global economy recovery. Based on this good news and encouraging expectations, the fund may soon get some US$200 billion from the PBoC currency reserves, according to the *Financial Times*[82].

Transparency

According to Truman's scoreboard, CIC was not transparent, with a rating of 29 out of 100. For its behaviour on reporting and defining its portfolio it received a very low rating. However, the Linaburg-Maduell Index improved its rating from six out of ten in 2008 to seven out of ten in 2009 in recognition of the fund's efforts to improve its transparency level. While before the CIC did not provide any public reporting, except for its report to the state council, following its participation in the IWG and the drafting of the Santiago Principles, in August 2009 the CIC launched its first annual report for the year 2008, approved by the board of directors and available on the fund's institutional website. The report also included 2008 financials and was prepared in accordance with the China Accounting Standards for Business Enterprises issued by the ministry of finance in 2006, which comply with International Financial Reporting Standards (IFRS).

While the CIC was opaque, significant concerns spread among Western governments and public opinion. The primary cause for concern was national security in certain sensitive sectors. The question was whether the CIC was motivated by commercial goals or geopolitical ones, aiming to gain controlling/majority shares in such strategic sectors as transport, infrastructure, telecommunications, energy, defence and high-tech. Secondly, recipient countries were concerned about quasi-monopolistic practices on the markets. It was feared that CIC aimed to increase Chinese national companies' global market shares at the cost of companies from other countries through targeted acquisitions or through the blocking of undesirable mergers/acquisitions between competitors in support of its own leading national companies. However, the financial crisis, on one hand, made Western markets eager to receive injections of fresh capital and, on the other hand, the empirical evidence that CIC has hitherto not carried out hostile operations or invested where public opinion was adverse, have contributed to reducing scepticism towards CIC.

Other entities

In Chapter 2 we classified several entities belonging to the Chinese government as SWFs.

SAFE Investment Company is the subsidiary of the State Administration of Foreign Exchange (SAFE), which manages the official reserves of the PBoC. SAFE Investment Company, created in 1997 and endowed with assets of US$300 billion, became an active investor domestically as well as abroad, in order to find more profitable ways to invest reserves. SAFE has therefore succeeded in carving out a role for investing the part of the currency reserves that is not needed for monetary policy. It behaves de facto like a SWF. It acquired shares in three Australian banks, a 1.6% share of Total, the French petroleum company, 1% of British Petroleum, almost 1% of Royal Dutch Shell, Aviva and Prudential. It also holds shares in Rio Tinto, Tesco, BHP Billiton and Barclays. It also made significant investments in the UK equity market in 2008. Apart from its shareholdings, all of them of modest size and well diversified, most of SAFE Investment Company's portfolio consists of external debt securities. SAFE Investment Company has an extremely low level of transparency. The Linaburg-Maduell Index assigned it a rating of two out of ten in third-quarter 2009. The financial crisis also hit SAFE: it had indirectly invested US$2.5 billion via the TPG private equity fund in Washington Mutual bank (US), which went bankrupt in 2008. However, the Chinese government announced in April 2009 that its investments of foreign exchange reserves remained profitable in 2008 despite the global financial crisis.

Considering its nature as an implicit SWF, it is quite reasonable to imagine a strong rivalry between SAFE and CIC. The former's greater opacity could play to its favour, especially if the Chinese government feels constrained by the new transparency standards set by CIC. However, if the government assigns another tranche of official reserves to CIC, this will mark CIC's status as a major Chinese investor abroad.

Another Chinese SWF, according to our classification, is the National Social Security Fund, a US$114 billion pension fund of the SPRF-type, deriving its revenues from the privatisation of state-owned enterprises and other investment and fiscal proceeds. Established in 2000, only in 2006 was it authorised to invest 20% of its capital endowment abroad. Its investment is done mainly through intermediaries with the mandate to invest abroad in shares and securities. The National Social Security Fund is managed by a state ministerial agency directly controlled by the state council. As a pension fund, it is more transparent than SAFE, with a rating of 77 on Truman's scoreboard and five out of ten in 2009 according to the Linaburg-Maduell Index. In its annual report for 2008, it recorded its first annual loss (of 6.8%) since its founding. In 2009, the fund prepared to increase private equity investments in view of the enlargement of the total size of its assets to US$146 billion.

Another SWF active in China is the Investment Portfolio of the Hong Kong Monetary Authority. This institution, founded in 1993, acts to stabilise monetary policy and invests mainly in the domestic market, the Hang Seng. The Investment Portfolio division, created in 1998 and endowed with US$140 billion, can be considered a SWF authorised to invest its assets abroad, including in stocks. Its goal is to ensure long-term purchasing power of the fund's assets. Its transparency level is quite high: Truman's scoreboard assigns it 67 out of 100 and the Linaburg-Maduell Index rates it eight out of ten in 2009.

There are also many Chinese former state-owned companies with enough resources to make foreign acquisitions. In addition they have easy access to public financing. Chinese banks, which enjoy a protected regime and have accumulated significant profits, are also capable of investing these profits abroad – as exemplified by the Industrial and Commercial Bank of China, which bought 20% of Standard Chartered Bank. It is no coincidence that the CIC hurried to acquire significant shares in the major Chinese banks so as to also be able to act indirectly, inducing banks to finance foreign acquisitions or support Chinese companies investing abroad.

According to some critics, in this mass of operations it is possible to distinguish not so much a strategic plan but the overlapping of different political powers and the long-standing dispute between the ministry of finance and the PBoC for control over the management of reserves. Proof of this can be found in SAFE's attempt to expand its foreign investments, thus occupying the same space as CIC.

The total volume of foreign direct investment (FDI) by Chinese public and private companies equals US$82 billion over the past ten years and it is plausible that most of these investments came from state-owned entities. If US$82 billion still appears modest compared to total global FDI, this sum nevertheless epitomises the impressive effort China is making to go global. In our opinion, the initiatives summarised in this paragraph are part of this effort. They represent the initial stage of a broader foreign investment strategy which in the second decade of the 21st century could make China into one of the world's largest foreign investors.

Norway: Government Pension Fund-Global (GPF-G)

Type, ownership and size

GPF-G was the first SWF established in Europe, set up in 1990 by the parliament of Norway to invest wealth generated from oil extraction and in particular from:

- taxing oil companies

- extraction rights

- dividends from the partially state-owned company Statoil Hydro.

Initially called the Petroleum Fund of Norway, in 2006 it was renamed the Norway Government Pension Fund-Global. Although this is not a pension fund in the classic sense, as its financing does not derive from pension contributions, one of its principle purposes was and still is to pay for the growing cost of public pensions. The Government Pension Fund-Global (GPF-Global) belongs to the category of sovereign pension reserve funds (SPRF) according to the definition provided in the second chapter. As such it falls under the definition of a SWF.

GPF-G received its first transfer from the Norwegian government in 1996, since the first budget surplus was achieved in 1995. Subsequent years were richer and this allowed the fund to grow well beyond Norwegian GDP; it is forecast to reach 250% of GDP by 2030.

In terms of size, GPF-G is the second largest SWF in the world and the largest in Europe, with US$431 billion in assets as of September 2009[83]. It is wholly owned by the Norwegian government through the ministry of finance. In terms of transparency, it is considered a benchmark; its characteristics are deemed best practices by international standards.

Objectives and organisation

GPF-G's stated objectives are threefold: firstly, to ensure that a substantial part of the wealth generated by oil goes to future generations in anticipation of the depletion of this raw material; secondly, to facilitate the accumulation of financial assets to cope with future pension outlays in anticipation of the growing social security costs due to an ageing population; and thirdly to counterbalance the effects of the fluctuation in the price of crude oil.

A long-term vision prevails in assessing investments and particular emphasis is placed on the concept of economically, environmentally and socially sustainable development.

The governance structure is well defined and clearly delineates the division of responsibilities between the political authorities and operational management. The formal owner of the fund is the ministry of finance. The fund's management and the definition of its strategic objectives and risk parameters are the responsibility of the ministry of finance. In turn the ministry of finance has delegated the fund's operational management to the Norwegian Central Bank (Norges Bank) through its subsidiary Norges Bank Investment Management

(NBIM), an operational investment management unit established in 1998 and responsible for investing GPF-G's assets internationally. The ministry reports data on the fund's management and its investments directly to parliament.

The fund is integrated into the state budget: deficits can go to diminishing the GPF-Global when needed. Government withdrawal requires a parliamentary vote.

The fund attributes particular importance to ethical norms, and the respect of Norwegian international obligations deriving from international treaties emphasising Norway's commitment to global justice.

Ethical considerations are given effect in three specific ways:

1. active exercise of ownership rights

2. negative screening of companies

3. exclusion of those companies from the fund's portfolio deemed to violate ethical guidelines.

Concerning the first point, NBIM exercises active shareholder rights on behalf of GPF-G and complies with internationally accepted principles such as the UN Global Compact and the OECD Guidelines of Corporate Governance for Multinational Enterprises. Through active management and ownership it is possible to pursue two goals at once: promoting the financial interests of the fund's owners and ensuring that company behaviour is in line with the shareholders' ethical principles.

Concerning the second and third points, we must analyse the process of establishing ethical guidelines and the creation of the council on ethics.

In 2004, ethical guidelines were defined based on the recommendations of a government commission. According to the guidelines, the fund may not invest in companies which, directly or via subsidiaries:

- seriously or systematically violate human rights (i.e. murder, torture, deprivation of liberty, forced labour, the worst forms of child labour and other child exploitation)

- seriously violate individuals' rights in situations of war and conflict

- cause severe environmental damage

- practise gross corruption

- seriously violate other fundamental ethical norms.

The ethics guidelines are enforced by a council on ethics, an independent advisory body established by royal decree in 2004, in charge of assessing whether or not a company ought to be excluded from investment by the Government Pension Fund-Global, based on the above principles.

The council consists of five members (three academics at the University of Oslo, a professional scientist and a professional economist) who assess whether an investment target is compatible with the fund's ethical guidelines. The ministry of finance may request the council's opinion or the council may act autonomously in issuing a recommendation not to invest in a company.

The company under scrutiny shall receive the recommendation and the reasons for it and has the opportunity to comment on the charge. A significant portion of the investigative work underpinning the council's recommendations is privatised. Specific organisations issue regular reports on companies, based on daily news and other research activities. However, the actual investigation is carried out by the council.

When the council issues a recommendation not to invest in a company it is submitted to the ministry of finance, which has the final say on the matter and normally follows the council's recommendations. The ministry's decision and the council's recommendations are transparent and publicly available on the fund's website. Given the fund's size and the commonly shared principles upon which an exclusion is based, the process of "naming and shaming"[84] can produce headlines around the world, thus damaging the public image of the company in question.

Exclusion does not end the investigative work and the council regularly reviews whether the conditions for a specific company's exclusion still remain. If not, the council may recommend to the ministry of finance to revoke the exclusion. According to some authors, exclusion may be considered an incentive for the target company to change its behaviour[85]. Others maintain that exclusion has to do with the concept of avoiding complicity and is not intended to influence behaviour[86].

By 2008, 30 companies had been excluded out of a total of 7000 in the fund's portfolio[87]. The reasons for excluding companies were:

- production of cluster munitions (nine companies)

- production of nuclear weapons or components (ten companies)

- breaches of human rights (two companies)

- environmental damage (four companies)

- environmental damage and breaches of human rights (three companies)

- supply of arms or military equipment to Burma (one company)

- anti-personal landmines (one company).

Several other companies have been under scrutiny but did not end up being excluded. A few of them, after having been excluded, were reinstated when the reason(s) for exclusion ceased to exist.

Portfolio and main shareholdings

The fund invests in global markets in a wide range of financial instruments from fixed income securities to quoted shares, money market funds and derivatives in order to diversify its portfolio and maximise returns in correspondence with an acceptable level of risk. It does not invest in private equity.

The fund's strategic benchmark allocation is as follows:

- 60% in equities, of which 50% is in European stock markets, 35% in US and African stock markets and 15% in Asian stock markets

- 40% is in fixed income securities, of which 60% must be in European currencies, 35% in American currencies, 5% in Asian currencies.

Shareholdings have an exclusively financial purpose and are therefore always minority stakes. The quota limit for purchase of shares was raised by parliament in June 2008 from 5% to 10%. Through its manager, NBIM, the fund regularly exercises its right to participate and vote in annual shareholders' meetings of the companies in which it holds shares. The 2008 annual report signalled that the fund voted on more than 68,000 items at more than 7,500 annual meetings around the world.

In 2008 the fund made record purchases in equity markets. In 2009 GPF-G held shares in approximately 7,900 companies, representing on average 1% of the world's listed companies. The ten most significant ones as of September 2009 were: HSBC Holdings (UK), Royal Dutch Shell (UK), Nestlé (Switzerland), British Petroleum (UK), Total (France), Banco Santander (Spain), Telefónica (Spain), Vodafone (UK), Exxon Mobil (US) and Roche Holding (Switzerland). Its main shareholdings are heavily concentrated in Europe in various sectors, primarily energy and utilities, financial and telecoms. As for its fixed income securities, the most significant are mainly US, European and Japanese public debt securities.

GPF-G allocates a variable quota of its portfolio to external asset managers chosen on the basis of purely financial criteria. This percentage can vary: in September 2009 it was 13% of the fund's assets, but it can easily reach one-third of the total portfolio.

The annual return at the end of 2008 on a yearly basis was highly negative at -23.3% in international currency, the worst result in the fund's history (in 2007 the yearly return had been +4.26%) and 3.4 percentage points lower than the return on the benchmark portfolio. The presence in the portfolio of Lehman Brothers stocks and bonds and Fannie Mae and Freddie Mac bonds contributed to worsening an already serious situation for the year dominated by the financial global crisis. On a ten-years basis the annual return went down to 2.33% from 6.29% in 2007. In 2009 performance considerably improved and returns rebounded, reaching 13.5% on a quarterly basis, the best quarterly result ever (with an excess return of 1.5% on the benchmark portfolio). This translated into a yearly return of 9.2% on the previous year and 3.94% over the past ten years.

During the global financial crisis the fund became keener to support domestic economic programs and part of the fund was used to finance a domestic stimulus package.

Transparency

GPF-Global claims the important standing of being the most transparent SWF of this size in the world. Truman's scoreboard assigns it a rating of 92 out of 100, in third place after the Alaska Permanent Fund and New Zealand's Superannuation Fund, far smaller SWFs. In terms of reporting and governance, the Norwegian fund has the best all-round rating. The Linaburg-Maduell Index gives it the maximum score of ten and used it as a benchmark in creating the index. In defining its principles of good conduct for SWFs, the IMF's International Working Group considered it a reference point.

GPF-Global produces annual and quarterly reports on investment strategies and goals, portfolio assets, investments made and withdrawn, results and performance, risk, and balance sheet data. These reports are available to the public on the internet. The fund also publishes detailed information on the fund's voting in shareholder meetings.

According to some commentators, the Norwegian fund is paradoxically the most striking example of a large fund acting not only on the basis of financial but also political criteria. The ethical guidelines introduce a value-based dimension that has little to do with maximising financial returns. This produces a certain ambivalence: the fund declares it operates like a private investor seeking to maximise shareholder value, but this also entails acting to maximise the influence of shareholders' moral values[88]. On the one hand it has an image of the perfect private investor, and on the other hand it consciously pursues state policy targets aimed at projecting Norwegian values in the world. GPF-G demonstrates that sovereign investors, even if completely transparent and organised on the basis of private investor models, may always behave as political subjects. Seeking to influence not only individual companies but also whole industries and countries, it can be argued that the fund's management is as much about political activity – albeit arguably benign – as financial management[89].

However, in line with the Santiago Principles (in particular GAPP number 19), we think that what really matters is not necessarily behaving according to criteria for financial maximisation, but making transparent any other consideration that might motivate a fund/investor's decisions. If criteria other than economic and financial goals inspire SWFs, they should be clearly set up and publicly disclosed. And this is certainly the case with GPF-G.

Russia: RF and NWF

Type, ownership and size

The Russian Reserve Fund (RF) and National Wealth Fund (NWF) are both owned by the Russian Federation and originated from the recent division in January 2008 of the Oil Stabilization Fund, the forerunner of Russia's current SWFs.

The Oil Stabilization Fund, established in January 2004, was managed by the minister of finance and was the holder of taxes deriving from oil extraction. It was conceived as a stabilisation fund with the scope of insulating the economy from the volatilities of oil revenues. This appeared quite reasonable, taking into account that in 2008 oil revenues represented roughly 70% of Russian exports and 50% of fiscal income[90]. When the oil price exceeded US$27 a barrel (since 2006; in 2004 and 2005 the threshold price was US$20), reserves accumulated in the fund. If the oil price was below this threshold, the government had the right to draw directly from the fund to address public expenditures and balance the state budget deficit. Since 2004, rising oil prices caused the fund to grow beyond all expectations, reaching US$157 billion in January 2008[91]. This amount is even more impressive if we consider that part of the fund's assets have been used to repay debts contracted abroad (loans from the IMF and the countries of the Paris Club for US$15 billion in 2005 and US$23 billion in 2006) and to finance agencies for economic development (US$26 billion in 2007).

As a result of the division in January 2008, the RF was endowed with US$125 billion and the NWF with US$32 billion.

On 1 December 2009 the two funds had combined assets of US$168 billion, of which US$93 billion belonged to the NWF and US$75 billion to the RF.

The real stabilisation fund substituting the Oil Stabilization Fund is the RF. It differs from the past arrangement mainly due to the fact that the RF functions as a stabilisation fund not only with oil revenues, but also with proceeds from natural gas.

Objectives and organisation

The RF's objective is to ensure that state budget expenditures are financed and that the budget remains balanced even when oil and gas prices drop. If expenditures exceed energy revenues, funds can be taken from the RF. Otherwise when energy revenues exceed budget requirements, the excess revenue is credited to the RF up to a maximum ceiling of 10% of GDP. Essentially the RF's purpose is to insulate the economy from the volatility of oil and gas prices and to absorb excess liquidity, thus reducing inflationary pressures. Any further surplus revenues are given to the NWF. The NWF's objective is to co-finance a pension system for Russian citizens and keep Russia's actual pension fund balanced. This fund is similar to the Norwegian Government Pension Fund and it can therefore be classified as a sovereign pension reserve fund (SPRF), which we consider an SWF.

The RF and the NWF are both managed by the minister of finance. Some management functions are delegated to the Russian central bank, which is also the depository of the funds' assets until a new dedicated state agency is set up to manage Russian public funds. The creation of such an agency under the name of Russian Financial Agency was announced in January 2009, but not implemented.

Portfolio and main shareholdings

The RF and the NWF have different investment policies. The NWF's risk profile is higher than the RF's since the former may also invest in corporate bonds and shares. Moreover, the NWF has a longer-term investment horizon than the RF.

The RF invests in debt securities of foreign government (95% of total portfolio) and of international financial organisations (5%)[92].

The issuers of these securities may not have a rating of less than AA- or Aa3 confirmed by at least two rating agencies. The currency composition must be 45% in US dollars, 45% in euros and 10% in pounds sterling.

The NWF invests both in foreign currency and Russian rubles and in particular in debt securities of foreign states (100% of foreign currency portfolio) and in deposits in state corporation banks (100% of ruble-denominated portfolio)[93].

The RF's rules regarding rating of issuers and currency composition also apply to the NWF.

The main difference between the two funds consists of the NWF's authorisation to invest up to 50% of its portfolio in equities in both foreign currency and rubles. However, this possibility has not yet been exploited and the ministry of finance decided to allocate the whole portfolio in foreign currency to state debt securities and to deposit the whole portfolio in rubles at the Vnesheconombank (VEB), the fourth-largest Russian bank, used as a channel to transmit public aid to Russian banks and firms during the financial crisis. Up to December 2009, US$18 billion was deposited at VEB (at an interest rate of 7%) to be lent to Russian banks, while another US$4 billion were used to support Russian financial markets buying of shares and bonds. In January 2010 a loan of another US$2 billion (with interest of 2.75 percentage points above the London interbank offered rate) was granted to the same bank to finance infrastructure projects[94].

Until recently, the Russian funds were considered among those with the greatest growth potential. This was due to the dynamics of energy raw materials prices, their source of financing. However, with the fall in the price of oil and the unfolding of the 2007-2009 financial crisis, these forecasts were greatly reduced. This crisis caused significant damage in Russia, including closure of the Moscow stock exchange for several days and liquidity problems for Russian banks. In response, the financial resources of the funds were directed to domestic use; and, for a while, would not be invested abroad.

Several legal modifications[95] were passed in order to make it easier to deploy fund reserves for domestic use. Starting in 2009 and lasting until 2012, the government is not required to change federal law in order to use the RF's assets to finance the budget deficit and repay public debt. The RF can be used to finance not only federal but also regional budget deficits. If the oil price goes below US$70 a barrel, the RF can be tapped without consulting parliament. From 1 January 2010 to 1 February 2012, returns from the RF and NWF asset management will not be reinvested in the fund but will be deployed to finance state budget expenditures.

As a result, according to the minister of finance, the RF will dry up by 2010 if the budget deficit remains high (7.4% of GDP in 2009)[96].

The two funds proved to be important assets to support the Russian economy during the financial crisis: the RF was used to tap budget deficits, while the NWF was used to support the financial system and the stock exchange. However, if this situation continues for the long term, it is doubtful that either fund will remain definable as a SWF.

Transparency

According to Truman's scoreboard the level of transparency for the two Russian funds is 51 out of 100. The Linaburg-Maduell Index gives them a rating of five out of ten in third-quarter 2009.

The minister of finance must provide the government with quarterly data on accumulation, investments, usage and value of assets for both funds. In turn the government is obliged to render an account on a yearly basis of the same points to parliament. At the beginning of each month the minister of finance must publish a report for the media on accumulation, expenditures and investments for both funds. These financial statements are subject to an annual audit by a board of auditors which is public, but formally independent[97]. The transparency level in terms of reporting and auditing procedures can be deemed satisfactory. However, considering the important role of the two funds in supporting Russian banks and firms in the crisis and considering the close linkages in Russia between economics and politics, a significantly higher level of transparency would be desirable in terms of the firms receiving financial support and Russian shares and bonds being acquired on the stock exchange. Otherwise the risk of spending resources from oil in favour of a few oligarchs may become real. Paradoxically, in the case of the Russian funds, instead of being worried about them possibly entering Western companies with strategic targets, the main concern now relates to the best domestic usage of oil revenues.

4.

Strategies and Effects on Global Financial Markets

The size of SWF assets, their concentration in a few organisations with strong decision-making powers, and their geopolitical locations are all elements that need to be looked at in terms of SWF behaviour on international financial markets. We will address the most important questions that arise when doing so.

- What are the strategies of SWFs on international markets?

- Do they operate with economic-financial and/or political-strategic motivations, and what have been the results and effects of their behaviour?

- Are SWFs stabilising or destabilising agents in international financial markets?

It is important not to be limited to mere anecdotes in understanding the above, so the detailed analysis that follows will refer to and compare economic research that has been carried out on the topic so far.

Strategies on International Markets

The poor transparency of most SWFs, the relatively brief period of their global prominence and the high differentiation between funds makes it difficult to evaluate with certainty any aggregate strategy. As a rule, owners of huge financial resources who are not seeking to acquire controlling stakes in companies try to combine risk and return with a diversified allocation between financial instruments, geographical areas, currencies, sectors, and time horizons. In this sense SWFs have made 'normal' choices, but they have also made 'anomalous' ones in terms of the return-risk balance.

Naturally the strategies chosen depend on the type of SWF. They differ significantly in terms of asset allocation, risk-management strategies and investment horizons as a consequence of their different purposes and constraints. Stabilisation funds, for example, with medium-term horizons, tend to invest in less risky liquid instruments; in contrast, savings funds for future generations and pension funds have longer-term horizons and prefer riskier financial instruments with higher returns.

In this chapter we draw on various sources. In particular we will refer to the reports edited by Monitor Group together with Fondazione Eni Enrico Mattei (FEEM) on the basis of the Monitor-FEEM SWF Transaction Database, and to various studies by Steffen Kern of Deutsche Bank Research. Both have used publicly reported transactions that could represent only 10-20% of the total amount of transactions undertaken by SWFs, a relatively small percentage. This happens because some transactions are anonymous investments in liquid assets, or because third parties (asset managers) are used to act on the behalf of SWFs. As the rest of SWF transactions are completely unknown, we have no other choice but to study SWFs based on this narrow foundation of data. The prevalence of anonymous investments and the use of asset managers are also reasons why only a few of ADIA's transactions are recorded, while the Norwegian GPF-G has no records at all. It must also be noted that the underlying SWF classification – which the extractions from the two databases are based on – not only differs slightly between the two, but also as compared to our classification in Chapter 2. In spite of these limits, though, the data we present here does capture the macro trends that characterise the strategies and behaviour of SWFs on financial markets. And this is supported by the fact that their outcomes converge on most of the issues.

The Monitor-FEEM SWF Transaction Database includes 1,158 publicly disclosed investments in listed and unlisted companies, real estate and private equity funds performed by SWFs between January 1981 and December 2008 for a total value of US$370 billion. Although this database does not include all transactions carried out by SWFs, it is one of the largest and most comprehensive sources of SWFs' investments existing today.

According to Miracky and Bortolotti[98], who use the Monitor-FEEM SWF Transaction Database, investments by SWFs peaked in 2008 at 175 transactions worth a total of US$128 billion. 2008 can be considered a watershed for SWF activity. While the first half of the year was characterised by an investment boom (the first quarter accounts for a third of the year's deals and half their value), in the second quarter of 2008 investments started to decrease, declining by almost 50% by number and 14% in value terms compared to the previous quarter. This sharply contrasted with 2007, when SWFs concluded 161 deals for a total value of US$102 billion in an increasing trend from the first to the last quarter. In 2005 and 2006, while the number of deals was high (143 and 135 respectively), the value, albeit on the increase, was still far below the explosion of 2007 that saw a doubling of the 2006 value. The overall balance of 2008 is still positive, indicating an increase on 2007, although a slowdown was already apparent. This phase of retrenchment appeared to come to an end only in the third quarter of 2009, when there was a considerable upswing in SWF activity[99]. The financial tsunami thus did not determine the end of SWFs, but it certainly contributed to a review of investment strategies in order to adapt to a new financial scenario.

Figure 7 – SWF investments over time (number and value in US$ billion)

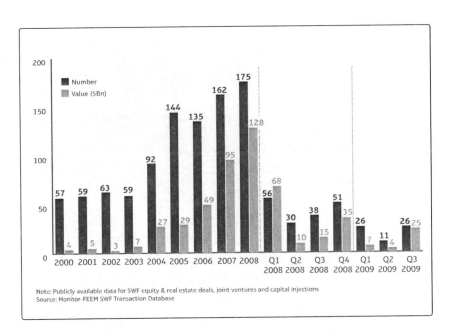

Source: Miracky, Barbary, Fotak and Bortolotti (2009) on Monitor-Feem SWF Transaction Database.

Kern[100] arrives at the same conclusions using a more limited database[101], including SWF transactions over the period 1995-June 2009 for a total of US$185 billion in publicly listed companies. He finds a strong acceleration in the period 2004-2008 and a particular emphasis on the financial sector in the years 2007-2008. In 2009 the pace of investments slowed, decreasing by 50% on 2008. In 2009 the financial sector lost its allure. Between end-2008 and beginning-2009 many funds shifted the focus of their investments to domestic markets, suspending or cutting investments abroad.

Figure 8 – SWF investments over time (US$ billion)

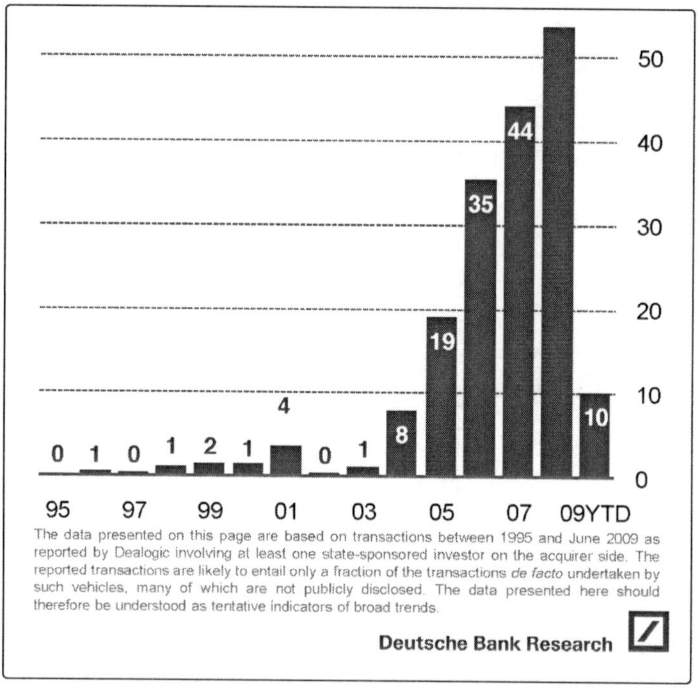

Source: Kern (2009) (Deutsche Bank Research) on data Dealogic.

The geographic map of investments

According to Kern[102], the most active SWFs classified by origin are those of Asia. Their US$79 billon represents 43% of the total amount of transactions reported by the Dealogic database from 1995 to June

2009. These are followed by the Middle Eastern funds with US$53 billion, representing 29% of the total, and other regions with the remaining US$52 billion, representing 18% of the total.

When the same transactions are classified by geographical destination, the main target markets for SWF stock capital investments are: Asia with US$58 billion or 31% of all transactions, the EU with US$57 billion or 30%, the US with US$37 billion or 20% and the other regions with the remaining US$34 billion or 19%. In Europe, the United Kingdom attracts most of the investments for US$28 billion or about half of the total invested in the EU. This is consistent with the importance of transactions in the financial sector. The second most popular country, Germany – with about US$8 billion in investment, or 15% out of the total EU investments – is far behind.

Figure 9 – Geographical destination of SWF investments: 1995 to June 2009 (US$ billion and % of total)

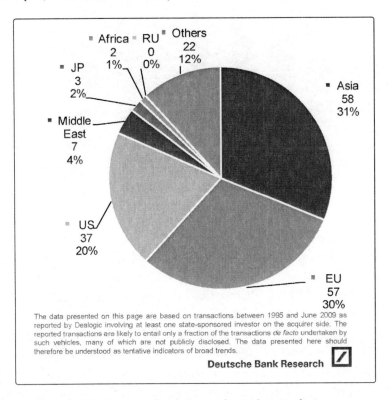

Source: Kern (2009) (Deutsche Bank Research) on data Dealogic.

According to Miracky and Bortolotti[103], there was an increasing shift in the focus of SWF investments from international to domestic markets during 2008. This reached its peak in the last quarter of the year, with almost US$79 billion directed to domestic markets (representing 26% of all the transactions undertaken during the year and 43% of transactions in the quarter). This marks a reversal in comparison with the continuous trend of declining domestic investment since 2002. This trend reversed again in 2009[104], when almost all transactions were international. This confirms the tendency of SWFs to seek international investments much more than domestic ones.

Figure 10 – Number of SWF deals: domestic vs foreign

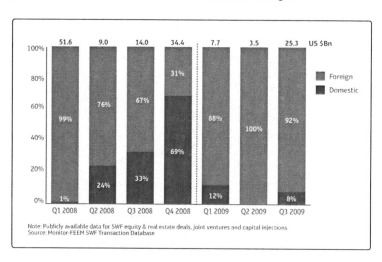

Source: Miracky, Barbary, Fotak and Bortolotti (2009) on Monitor-Feem SWF Transaction Database.

In 2008, emerging markets increased their importance as destinations for SWF investments to the detriment most of all of the US and Europe. Whilst in terms of value of SWF investments received, the OECD prevailed (US$87 billion); in terms of the number of deals, emerging markets took the lead, with 99 deals or 57% of the total. Among emerging economies, those of Asia have proven the most attractive[105]. The OECD regained its edge in the last part of 2009, when it received almost 90% of the value of all transactions. Europe led the rank, with US$17 billion representing 40% of all transactions. This marked the continent's best performance in two years, and testifies to the belief of SWFs in the positive long-run outlook of the European economy.

In terms of geographic origin, according to Miracky and Bortolotti[106] the most active investors are Asia-Pacific-based, representing 70% of the number of deals and 62% of the value over the entire period 1981-2008. The leading SWFs in terms of number of transactions are Temasek (43% of the total), GIC (16%) and Khazanah (9%). In terms of value CIC leads the rank with US$82 billion, followed by GIC (US$73 billion) and Temasek (US$56 billion). Among the Middle Eastern funds, the most active are Istithmar, Mubadala and QIA. These results may appear surprising due to the absence of the two largest SWFs: ADIA and Norwegian GPF-G. For the former there are a few transactions, while for the latter no records at all. The problem is that these SWFs sub-contract all or most of their investments to asset managers so their names never appear in any database. 2009, and in particular the last quarter of the year, was the year of CIC, while other normally active Asian funds such as those of Singapore were very quiet.

Figure 11 – Most active SWFs in the period 1981-2008

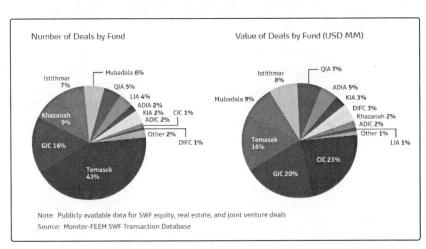

Source: Miracky and Bortolotti (2009), on Monitor-Feem SWF Transaction Database.

Christopher Balding[107] shows with Bloomberg and Thomson One Banker data related to the major SWFs that most of them, whilst investing internationally, invest mainly in regional markets, highlighting a tendency to not stray too far from home. The pattern of investing in the near abroad is more pronounced for the Asian funds: those in Singapore invested mainly within the city-state (65% of total share investments) and on the Asian continent; the Chinese CIC invested mostly in China, with its acquisitions in the banking sector. For these funds, investing in Europe and the United States could be considered a strategy of geographical diversification. The Norwegian fund invests mainly in Europe and has stated a clear preference for developed countries. On the other hand, SWFs from the Middle East have always preferred the United States and the EU, and in particular the UK, also due to the lack of investment opportunities in their domestic and regional markets. In the last year, however, these funds appear to be turning increasingly towards their own regional emerging markets.

Another study by Chhaochharia and Laeven[108] reveals the same trends. Data gathered on 30,000 equity investments showed that SWFs tend to invest in countries that share similar cultural traits. While this tendency is common to other global investors, cultural bias for SWFs seems particularly pronounced. This can be explained by the preference of SWFs to invest in the familiar (raising doubts about compliance with the principles of portfolio theory), or attempts to exploit informational advantages.

The sectoral map of investments

Referring again to Kern[109], it turns out that the financial sector has absorbed the lion's share of SWF investments (for the period 1995 to 31 July 2009) with US$78 billion, representing 42% of the total. These investments peaked in the period end-2007-2008.

The same trend is confirmed by Miracky and Bortolotti[110], according to whom the peak period was the first quarter of 2008 when SWFs spent US$58 billion on Western financial institutions (GIC and KIA being the main players). Investments in the financial sector represented 96% of the total value of that year. The surge of investment in the financial sector was a recent phenomenon: in 2006 this sector attracted only less than one-fifth of SWF investments and still less in the previous years. Between 1986 and 2008 the financial sector represented just under one-third of the number of deals and more than half of SWF investments in value terms.

This could be considered an anomalous choice due to the large concentration of risk it involved. However, some reasons can be adduced to explain it. The first relates to the sector's profitability. Until the crisis spread, there were expectations of large profits as the sector's historic ROEs (returns on equity) up until 2006 were around 17% in Europe and 12% in the US. The fall in share prices during the crisis presented opportunities for what appeared to be exceptionally cheap acquisitions. The second reason was political-strategic. This was an opportunity to comprehensively enter the financial sector, the importance of which was clear for the international positioning of SWF. A third reason was pressure by Western governments and financial institutions in calling on SWFs to bail out their banks.

This opportunity was enhanced by the fact that in the recipient countries, under pressure from the crisis, attitudes toward SWFs completely changed. Funds that previously had been viewed with distaste were warmly welcomed as stabilising agents in the markets, with enough liquidity to rescue some of the investment banks in serious trouble. In this way SWFs were able to clear up their image in front of Western policymakers and companies. All of this led to SWFs holding significant stakes in important Wall Street and European banks[111]. In order not to disturb Western sensitivities, SWFs limited themselves to minority positions, almost never exceeding 10%, and at times investing in stocks without the right to vote. In all cases they did not request positions on boards of directors or participate in strategic or operational decisions in the held companies.

The boom of SWF investment in the financial sector ran out of steam, however. The real watershed was the collapse of Bear Sterns in March 2008. In early 2010, except for QIA's investment in Barclays in June 2008, and Temasek's in Merrill Lynch in July 2008, no major further investments had taken place since the second quarter of 2008.

This reversal happened for at least three reasons.

1. An excessive concentration of risk in a sector which incurred a drastic fall in stock prices led to losses exceeding 80% of acquisition prices at the lowest point, even if they were not realised.

2. Uncertainty hanging over the entire banking and financial sector and in particular the investment banks; they have almost disappeared in the US, and therefore globally, due to mergers with and incorporations by commercial banks.

3. Massive government capital interventions, with the resulting substantial change in the nature of these banks.

In 2009, bank share prices recovered somewhat, thus alleviating attributed losses. If SWFs held on to their shareholdings with a long-term view, and if stock markets continued to rebound, final realised losses could yet be minimised. Since SWFs are not subject to pension withdrawals or other liquidity constraints and in most cases are not exposed to high leverage ratios, they were in a position to wait until market conditions improved.

SWF investments in other sectors in 2009 were as follows[112]. Investments in the manufacturing industry recorded a total of US$25 billion or 14% of the total, followed by services and retail sector with nearly US$24 billion, representing 13% of the total. Then came real estate, for US$21 billion, representing 11% of the total, followed by the energy and raw materials sector with US$18 billion or 10%. Finally we find the technology sector (IT, telecoms and aerospace), defence and others, each respectively with US$17 billion (9%), US$2 billion (1%) and US$0.3 billion. As can be noted, the defence sector, crucial from the security point of view, did not receive significant investment.

By combining geographic and sectoral dimensions it is possible to trace the even distribution of sectors of sovereign investment in the EU with the sole exception of finance, which represented 41% and was essentially directed to the UK. In the US the percentage going to the financial sector was more significant, representing 59% of all inward SWF investment. This trend shows the financial sector decisively dominating investment patterns in the US, with much less balanced investment in other industries. The region where investments are more balanced is Asia, with only 15% of the total directed toward the financial sector and manufacturing being the primary target with 35%.

The trend toward sectoral diversification is destined to grow. SWFs have shifted their attention towards manufacturing, infrastructure, energy and natural resources and engineering-related sectors. This trend reflects a change in strategy: now the leading goals appear to be technology transfer and energy and commodity supplies that serve to better diversify and strengthen domestic economies.

Portfolio allocation in various financial instruments

Let us now look at the map of financial instruments in which SWFs invest. We will start with the survey conducted on SWFs in 2008 by the IMF's International Working Group (IWG)[113] in the form of a questionnaire on investment strategies to which about 20 funds responded, including the largest and most representative. The survey highlighted some variability in the type of financial instruments composing the portfolios of the SWFs which responded. SWFs range from those which prefer safe investments in highly rated government bonds, to others characterised by riskier strategies, with portfolios composed of 40-70% stocks, 4-10% private equity funds, 13-40% fixed income securities, 2-5% infrastructure investments, 2-5% raw materials, and 8-10% real estate investments.

The IWG study also revealed that all SWFs have fixed income securities in their portfolios, 60% have government securities, 40% have private equity stocks, 40% have real estate investments, and 30% have invested in raw materials. In addition, the following instruments are present in SWF portfolios: derivatives, private equity funds and hedge funds.

In spite of these highly different situations, with SWFs pursuing distinct investment strategies depending on their nature and scope, Kotter and Lel[114] sketched out a typical SWF portfolio: 35-40% composed of fixed income securities, 50-55% stocks, and 8-10% alternative investments including private equity funds, hedge funds, derivatives and raw materials.

We can thus conclude that the majority of SWFs show a preference for low-risk bonds, which are in fact present in all portfolios and represent the largest share in the majority of them. On the whole, the portfolios are sufficiently diversified, with a proper balance between stocks and fixed income, along with some alternative types of investments preferred primarily in the years running up to September 2008.

These estimates should nevertheless be taken with caution, not only due to the variety of possible situations but also because many funds do not publicise the compositions of their portfolios.

Other Market Strategies

Let us now consider the following aspects in terms of the market strategies of SWFs: a) defining investment goals; b) determining acceptable risk levels; c) operational management techniques such as the use of leverage and/or external managers, shareholding limits and the exercise of ownership rights, and other types of limits. We will use the IWG's survey for this[115].

1. In terms of defining investment objectives, 45% of those interviewed set relative objectives based on a reference benchmark; 30% set absolute return strategies; and 25% did not have detailed objectives but referred to the generic pursuit of long-term financial returns. Overall the majority (75%) set themselves specific objectives.

2. In terms of risk management, general goals are defined on an ownership level whereas specific ones are decided by management. The most common methods for covering risk are 65% based on credit ratings. Credit risk is limited due to the issuers' diversification. Liquidity risk is limited by the fact that the majority of securities held are quoted on regulated markets. Currency risk is limited based on theoretical maximum exposure.

3. The use of financial leverage is minimal, especially compared to financial institutions (which until recently reached ratios of 30%). Many funds are not even authorised to use financial leverage. 80% of the funds interviewed stated they did not use leverage directly; 20% use leverage indirectly by participating in funds which use it (hedge funds, for example); 30% use instruments based on leverage for coverage purposes. We can deduce that limiting or prohibiting the use of leverage does not mean not using it indirectly.

Regarding the use of external managers, most SWFs belonging to the sample of the IWG survey cited earlier appear to not use external managers. It would seem rational, however, to use external managers to deal with these dimensions since the expertise required is not easy to internalise. This is a rather differentiated type of policy, where the range of variation is quite high. However, Jen assumes that, in the aggregate, SWFs may out-place 20% or so of their assets with external investors[116]. 50% of the funds interviewed defined minimum acceptable rating limits of investments; 30% have limits on other portfolio features such as security currencies or destination countries of investment; 40% stated they have limits on the maximum share of ownership that can be held in the same company. The latter is a crucial point. It is possible to notice that, contrary to common belief, large-scale investments not only exist, but dominate[117]. In fact transactions of US$1 billion or higher represent 68% of the total and more than half of all the transactions involve a 20% stake in the target company (25% involve 100% control). Those data refer to publicly reported transactions and as such are biased towards large ones while undisclosed transactions, not included in this sample, are probably of a smaller size. Miracky and Bortolotti[118] confirm that SWFs tend to take controlling stakes, but this happens in emerging economies. In the OECD, and especially in sensitive sectors, SWFs avoid control. More than half of the transactions involving controlling stakes were undertaken by Asian SWFs, while Middle Eastern ones were less keen.

To conclude, in spite of the imbalance of SWFs in sectoral terms – with a marked preference for the banking-financial sector, for reasons we have seen – in terms of diversification of financial instruments and geographical areas, on average they appear to be economically rational investors guided by the goal of maximising returns in correspondence to acceptable levels of risk.

Effects on Financial Markets

Identifying the impact of SWF behaviour on financial markets is important. To evaluate this we will refer to a series of academic studies, based on market data, carried out between 2008 and 2009. What follows is not a mere academic exercise, but a necessary basis for quantitatively assessing the effects of SWFs on financial markets.

Beck and Fidora[119] propose a theoretical study based on the assumption of SWFs behaving as investors that allocate foreign assets according to market capitalisation rather than liquidity criteria. The authors assume the following currency composition of the reserve portfolios of emerging economies' central banks: 60.5% in US dollars, 28.6% in euros, 5.9% in pounds sterling, 2.6% in yen and 2.4% in other currencies. Under this assumption, the authors theorise a movement of assets from central banks' currency reserves to SWFs that will cause diversification of dollar- and euro-denominated (to a lesser degree) assets into those denominated in yen and emerging market currencies, causing net capital outflows from US and EU to emerging economies. This in turn would trigger movement from bonds to stocks. However, it must be noted that:

- central banks' choices to move currencies by central banks can only be implemented gradually and should be seen in light of SWFs not being able to easily disengage themselves from the dollar and euro as they are the cardinal currencies of the global economy

- a massive and concentrated flight from the dollar would entail undesirable effects for the exchange rate, which for many of the SWF home countries would be incompatible with their monetary and currency policy goals

- currency policies also take into account political relationships of power/coexistence between states and geopolitical areas.

The majority of SWFs are still anchored to the US dollar. This does not mean that emerging market currencies, especially Asian ones, are not destined to grow. But a shift by SWFs away from the dollar can only be gradual.

Investments/divestments of SWFs, similar to other large investors, have the potential to influence stock prices depending on the size and structure of these transactions and how they are communicated to or perceived by the market.

Recent papers analyse the impact of SWF investments on stocks, based on abnormal returns when SWF acquisitions are announced. Although the various authors use different samples, most of them find positive abnormal returns upon announcement of an SWF investment.

Kotter and Lel[120], based on a sample of 163 SWF investments (stock and fixed income) in 135 companies (taken from the Factiva database in the period 1980-2008) in 28 countries all over the world, find that markets react to SWF investments in the two days after the announcement with an average increase of 2.1% in risk-adjusted returns for the analysed stock. The announcement effect is statistically and economically significant. Moreover it is persistent, in the sense that these stocks continue producing abnormal returns for 20 days after the announcement. This means that the signals SWFs send to the market are significant. The effect of disinvestment was also measured on a smaller sample (12 companies), which showed a statistically significant negative impact confirming the previous analysis. The two authors also show that:

- the funds' level of transparency has a fundamental role in determining the market's reaction to an acquisition announcement. By using Truman's scoreboard from 2008, Kotter and Lel observed that the target companies undergo a greater average increase in returns when the fund is more transparent

- target companies' corporate governance, profitability and growth do not change significantly in the three years following investment by SWFs (for a controlled sample). This means that SWFs do not cause a long-term increase in the value of acquired companies, probably because they are passive investors.

Dewenter, Han and Malatesta[121], analysing a sample of 196 acquisitions and 47 divestments by SWFs in publicly traded shares, find abnormal positive and significant returns on the announcement date of SWF acquisition and negative returns when SWFs divest. This is in line with the previous study. These results are a non-monotonic function of the transaction size. For acquisitions, abnormal returns increase with the size of the transaction and, after reaching a peak, start to decrease. For divestments, abnormal returns decline first with the size of the transaction, reach a minimum and then increase. According to the authors this can be explained by a trade-off existing between the benefits, on the one hand, of monitoring activity on corporate governance – which more involved shareholders may carry out – and on the other, the loss of control that minority shareholders suffer when the majority shareholder is too powerful. They do not find convincing evidence that abnormal returns are systematically correlated with domestically-based target firms or with governance and transparency indicators (Truman index). In the long run the effect of acquisition is not statistically significant.

While the previous papers find significant abnormal returns upon announcement and no significant effects in the long run, in the following we will present some other works that reveal an impact on the target company's medium to long-term profitability.

Bortolotti, Fotak, Megginson and Miracky[122] use a sample of 235 investments by 21 SWFs in 195 publicly traded companies in the period between 1991 and 2008, drawing on the Monitor-FEEM SWF Transaction Database. Performing an event-study analysis, the authors find that the short-term impact of SWFs announcing an acquisition on target stocks causes a positive mean abnormal return of about 0.9% (in the three day interval including the announcement day) suggesting that investors view the arrival of SWFs positively. This reaction is stronger for the financial sector, signalling that SWF intervention is particularly appreciated when it is a bailout. On the contrary, abnormal returns of these stocks in the year following acquisition worsens (-15.49%) and this effect is more severe when large stakes are involved. In this study, therefore, SWFs have a negative impact on the acquired companies' medium-term profitability, suggesting that the monitoring effect is weak.

Chhaochharia and Laeven[123] reach the same conclusion, i.e. there is a positive market reaction when the acquisition by SWFs is announced, in part because these investments happen when firms are in financial distress, while in the long run the performance of the equity investment is poor.

Knill, Lee and Mauck[124] examine the impact of SWF investments on return and volatility using a sample of 232 SWF transactions. They find evidence of positive market reactions to announcements (1% abnormal return) consistent with Kotter and Lel (2008) and Dewenter et al (2009), while in the longer term they find negative abnormal returns which increase with longer horizons (16.6% lower 250 days after the announcement) consistent with Bortolotti et al (2009) and Chhaochharia and Laeven (2008). Overall they find small effects in the short term, but more significant negative effects in the long run. An event study was also done for sub-samples and revealed that the one-year abnormal return is -30.7% if SWFs are domiciled in oil-producing nations and -10% in other cases. This is probably due to the different media coverage of SWFs in those countries. The impact is -14.6% for opaque SWFs, while it is -20.6% for transparent ones. This means that domicile counts more than the level of transparency. Only non-financial targets showed a statistically significant decrease in abnormal returns, while financial ones did not. Finally there was a striking difference between transactions receiving media attention and those not receiving it, with a reduction of 27.1% for media-covered events versus 12.4% for non-media-covered ones (however, this could also be due to the fact that negative performance tends to receive more media attention). Concerning market volatility they find that a reduction in abnormal returns is accompanied by a reduction in volatility. However, risk reduction is not sufficient to offset the reduction in returns in order to preserve the return/risk relationship. This suggests that SWF investments could be potentially destabilising factors for financial markets.

All the above-cited studies converge on the positive short-term impact on stock prices of target companies following an announcement of acquisition by SWFs, while empirical evidence on the impact of acquisition by SWFs on the medium- and long-term performance of stocks is not univocal. This is understandable since, in the short term, SWF acquisitions convey positive information to investors, while in the long run the impact is subject to macroeconomic and financial conditions out of a fund's control, especially in cases of distressed companies (and also bearing in mind the reluctance of many SWFs to exercise shareholding rights and monitoring activity). While markets welcome the injection of liquidity from SWFs as contributing to price stabilisation, at the same time they are not convinced that SWFs alone can save the companies they are bailing out.

These results cannot be considered definitive since there are also studies that arrive at different conclusions. Sun and Hesse[125] perform a similar analysis, attempting to ascertain how stock markets react to the announcement of SWF investment by using an event-study approach. They base their study on 166 publicly disclosed investments/divestments by major SWFs in the period 1990-2009. They found that the short-term impact of the announcement varied according to different sectors (financial and non-financial), different markets (developed and emerging), level of corporate governance and type of action (investment or divestment), but overall that it did not result in any destabilising effect on equity markets measured in terms of abnormal returns.

Fernandes[126] takes a different approach, using a large data set of SWF shareholdings in more than 8,000 publicly traded firms (for a total of US$370 billion) in 58 countries in the period 2002-2007. He documents that SWF investments are associated with a significant premium – between 15% and 20% – of firm value, signalling that SWF ownership is positively valued by the market. Contrary to the previously cited articles, Fernandes bases his analysis on shareholdings instead of transactions. He also demonstrates that firms with higher SWF ownership have better operating performance. He finds a positive association between measures of operating profitability (return on assets (ROA), return on equity (ROE), and operating profit margins (EBITDA/sales and EBITDA/assets)) and a SWF stake of more than 1% in a firm. In this way he demonstrates that SWFs have a stabilising effect on markets and companies.

In a different setting, Bernstein et al[127] examine SWF private-equity investment strategies and how they are related to their organisational structure, in order to capture possible destabilising effects. They use a database of 2,662 transactions by 29 SWFs between January 1984 and December 2007. They find that SWFs invest at home when domestic equity prices are higher and invest abroad when foreign prices are higher. They invest at significantly lower price-earnings (P/E) ratios at home and higher P/E levels abroad. This is especially true for Asian and

Middle Eastern funds. Those same groups see the P/E ratios of investments at home fall in the year after the investment and increase when they invest abroad. Concerning the organisational structure, the authors show that the involvement of politicians determines a greater likelihood of investing domestically. SWFs with external managers tend to invest in industries with lower P/E ratios, while those with politicians involved tend to invest in industries with higher P/E ratios. SWFs with external managers see a more positive dynamic of P/E in the year after. On the contrary, funds with politicians involved see P/E ratios decrease the year after the deal. Those results support the idea that, when politics is involved, SWF performance worsens and this could generate distortions in investment decisions and therefore in financial markets with possible destabilising effects.

Another type of impact SWFs can have on the financial markets is on the average level of propensity for risk amongst operators, which in turn affects risk premiums. It is reasonable to assume that although SWFs have various risk strategies and propensities, they do contribute to an overall rise in the average propensity for risk on global financial markets. According to Jen and Miles[128], over the next ten years this will cause a reduction in stock returns and an increase in returns from fixed-income securities. Obviously these effects may be countered or aggravated by concomitant factors, including financial crises.

Evidence on the effects of SWFs on financial markets in terms of stabilisation/destabilisation is not yet conclusive since the various contributions present mixed results. However, destabilising effects, if any, seem to be rather limited, while a bias toward neutrality or slightly positive effects seems to prevail among the cited studies. More research is needed to provide an unambiguous answer to the question of whether SWF investment is beneficial or not for international financial markets.

Stabilising or worrying agents?

In order to understand the impact of SWFs on global markets, it is useful to summarise both their stabilising and worrying effects.

On the one hand, SWFs are recognised as contributing to the stability of the financial system due to their long-term horizons, the greater diversification of their portfolios, their average low level of indebtedness, and the absence of liquidity risks. As underlined by Gieve[129], if emerging countries' central banks decide to diversify their assets in search of higher returns, this should improve the efficiency of global asset allocation. Investing in equities in Western firms should also help to share a common interest in the good performance of companies they invest in and of the markets they operate in, thus encouraging the integration of emerging economies into the global economic system and policy making. Furthermore, during financial market downturns SWFs exhibited anti-cyclical behaviour: in 2000-2002 the Norwegian Government Pension Fund was a large buyer of global equities in a period when the equity market fell sharply and in 2008 SWFs invested in Western banks and financial companies in serious trouble, providing sought-after liquidity and contributing to easing financial market turmoil.

On the other hand, considering the size of SWFs and their consequent potential for imitative or anticipatory behaviour, their opacity, and the fact that they are not regulated, they can also act as destabilising factors for the markets. In addition, the fact that they are on average passive investors makes them relatively uninvolved in corporate management, which could negatively affect corporate governance in the held companies. Finally, due to the troubled reactions that SWFs often generate in the countries in which they invest, they could indirectly contribute to recent trends of de-globalisation and closure to foreign direct investment.

At least for now, empirical evidence seems to suggest that the stabilising factors outweigh the worrying ones, even if this evidence is not univocal and further research is required. However, when motivations are no longer related to profit maximisation but are of a political nature, the risk of distorting stock prices and the functioning of the market increases. Political motivations are not dangerous per se. They include, for example, the pursuit of economic diversification through a presence in basic industrial sectors, and the promotion of economic development. This can be considered legitimate and provides beneficial outcomes. However, political criteria certainly pose a challenge to global financial governance; such governance is designed on the basis of the assumption that actors pursue only sound economic returns. At this point, as the

Santiago Principles ask for in GAPP 19, transparency – within limits compatible with market competition – becomes essential for transforming a zero-sum game into a positive-sum game and helping to strike a stable and acceptable balance between host countries' legitimate security concerns and the global interest of maintaining open capital markets.

5.

Geoeconomics and Geopolitics

Recipient Countries' Concerns

SWFs can and must be seen not only from an essentially market-based perspective, as has been our approach up to now, but also from a geoeconomic and geopolitical one. The question is whether SWFs are changing or could change from portfolio investors, however important, to strategic players that influence an entire industry. Or could they even be arms of states which use them to influence other states? In other words, there are various related questions which move the attention from the economics to the politics of SWFs: their public nature; the more or less sensitive sectors in which they invest; their lack of transparency and sound governance practices; and their long-term strategies.

In this it is necessary, although not easy, to differentiate the facts as they are, from those that are likely in the future and those that are mere conjecture.

Let us start with the attention of international public opinion, which then turned into vigilance. One set of indicators consists of articles in periodicals. Looking at stories with headlines that include the words 'sovereign wealth funds', from 1 January 2008 to 31 December 2008, *The Economist* published more than 100 articles; on the *Financial Times* website there were 523 entries in 2007, 1,509 in 2008, and 560 in 2009. In 2008 the *Wall Street Journal* defined SWFs as "...one of the hottest topics in global financial markets"[130]. Prior to this there were practically no articles on this topic, indicating a peculiar inattention to a phenomenon that was already important and expanding.

The attention raised by SWFs has not only to do with the West's uneasiness in coping with the redistribution of financial and economic power to emerging countries (which SWFs symbolise as much as they embody). The list of concerns that have been raised in developed economies is much longer and stems from the worry that SWFs will be used to advance political agendas, thus representing a new form of state capitalism. In a frequently cited article[131], Lawrence Summers wrote that the concerns kindled by SWFs are profound and go to the nature of global capitalism itself: "The logic of the capitalist system depends on shareholders causing companies to act so as to maximise the value of their shares. It is far from obvious that this will over time be the only motivation of governments as shareholders." We are not sure that, after the global financial crisis, Summers would maintain such a clear conviction.

There is a long list of concerns about SWF investments on the part of recipient countries that can be classified into two broad groups: macro and micro risks.

The macro risks, which would mainly have an impact at the state level, include the following:

1. Owner states of SWFs could assume the power to negotiate the political future of countries in which they have invested, raising questions about national security, a multidimensional issue which changes from country to country.

2. The need to protect sectors (which have broadened with time) considered sensitive, from defence to energy, infrastructure, utilities, transport and extractive-mining.

3. The growing importance of SWFs could contribute to a change in the global geopolitical equilibrium between non-democratic states, where most of the SWFs are concentrated, and democratic states, where their investments are located.

4. The issue of appropriating technology and know-how in specific sensitive fields such as military technology and those critical for national security.

5. The risk of triggering a protectionist response toward foreign investment, contributing to the erection of protectionist barriers to capital flows.

The micro risks, which mainly have an impact at the company level – and risk distorting competition in international markets – include the following:

1. Owner countries of SWFs may promote their own national champions to the detriment of companies from countries in which they invest, weakening the competition with lawful and unlawful practices. The purpose of acquiring shares or investing in companies from other countries could be to weaken or control them in order to reinforce one's own state-owned companies to transform them from national state-owned champions into global champions, possibly with monopolistic powers.

2. Possible conflicts of interest between SWF owners and acquired companies or governments of countries in which they are investing. For example, if a country in need of raw materials acquires a company in that sector through its SWFs, that company's interest in keeping prices and profits high will conflict with the interests of the SWF owner country to reduce as much as possible the cost of raw materials.

3. SWFs could exercise their shareholders' controlling rights to accomplish political targets to the detriment of other shareholders' interests. In addition, in cases where they do not exercise control but hold significant shares, it is realistic to imagine that SWFs could exercise some influence.

4. State ownership of SWFs could reduce the efficiency of the companies in which they have invested, both because of political influence and because the necessary skills for managing the investments might be weak.

5. SWFs may give advantages to held companies on their own markets to the detriment of competing companies.

6. Controlled companies may be put in the position of competing on an unfair basis with other private companies, exploiting advantages deriving from their public nature, including the use of privileged information or the exercise of inappropriate influence.

7. The risk of corruption, which could cause emerging countries' assets to be misused or converted into personal wealth.

Possible concerns related to the functioning of financial markets will not be considered here since they have been covered in the previous chapter.

Influence on Western Democracies' Political Choices?

From the geopolitical-strategic point of view the interdependence of political and financial power is well known[132]. The central geo-strategic problem is the fact that a debtor's military and political power also depends on the support of its creditors. The more the United States relies on central banks and SWFs to finance its enormous deficit, the greater the risk of this limiting its political options. When it comes to making political choices or decisions to be taken by the UN Security Council, the United States cannot avoid taking into account the consequences of these choices for its public debt securities.

This is particularly worrying if one considers that owner countries of most SWFs are not democracies.

27 out of a total of 53 SWFs belong to states which have been defined as "authoritarian regimes" by *The Economist* Intelligence Unit's index of democracy[133]. Seven SWFs belong to "hybrid regimes". Another nine belong to states defined as "flawed democracies". Only ten belong to "full democracies". In terms of assets, 62% of SWF total assets are owned by authoritarian regimes, 18% by hybrid regimes, 2% by flawed democracies and 18% by full democracies. This is summarised in Figure 12.

The growing importance of authoritarian regimes does not only concern SWFs, but symbolises a broader shift of economic power. Growing global macroeconomic imbalances have contributed to shifting the balance of financial resources from Western countries (mostly democracies) to emerging countries (with different political regimes). This phenomenon can be illustrated by the evolution of current account surpluses, and distinguishing between "free", "partly free" and "not free" countries according to Freedom House country scoring[134]. Figure 13 shows how "not free" countries have accumulated current account surpluses at an astonishing pace, surpassing "free" countries.

Figure 12 – SWF assets and the political regimes of countries of origin

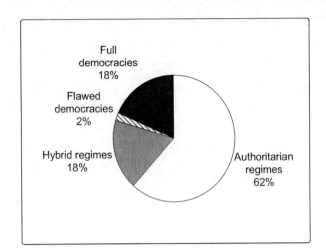

Source: Our elaborations on The Economist *Intelligence Unit's Index of Democracy 2008 and on Table 2.*

Figure 13 – Current account balances and political regimes

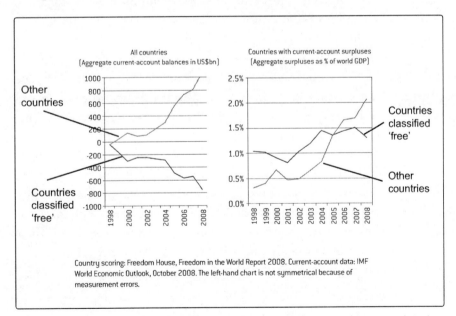

Source: Röller and Veron (2008), on Freedom House (World Report 2008) data and IMF (World Economic Outlook), October 2008.

Setser (2008a) shows how "liberal democracies" no longer hold the majority of foreign reserves, but these are now held by non-democratic regimes. The growth of foreign reserves owned by autocratic governments is also faster compared with the growth of those owned by liberal democracies.

The possibility of economic interdependence becoming a political lever has long been debated in the field of international relations. As Drezner points out[135], for financial statecraft to be effective, the creditor country should be much more powerful than the debtor one, and the former should be supported by a broad multilateral coalition in order to prevent other countries from intervening in the market and annulling the effect of financial threat. In addition, the danger of military conflict must be low. Apart from China and Russia, the owner countries of the main SWFs are small and more or less dependent on the United States: any attempt to use financial threats would generate greater costs than advantages and is thus highly unlikely. The likelihood that these countries could create a coalition is very small, since most of them have diverging interests.

Some authors (Drezner,[136] for example) have emphasised the negative political externalities SWFs could generate. We present them to provide a complete overview of the topic, but we consider these possibilities quite remote even if we are aware that they cannot be completely dismissed. For example, SWF home countries could start to be considered an alternative model to the Western democratic one based on rules and the market, thus attracting needy converts. In other words, the growing weight of some autocratic countries in global finance, combined with the growing fragility of international financial cooperation, could induce smaller countries in need of financing to follow alternative political models to democratic ones. Another way SWFs could damage democracy is that they strengthen the chances for survival of the regimes that created them, making it possible for their home countries to better defend themselves against economic crises before these regimes can be wiped out.

The overall risk is that Western democracies could lose their soft power along with control over international financial resources.

There is one more useful element to take into account in this analysis: the threat of using finance as a power lever by diversifying investments away from the large economies in order to damage exchange rates or cause interest rates to rise, is not credible at least in the short term for two reasons. First, it would be difficult for SWFs to find alternative markets for their huge amounts of capital (in some cases hundreds of billions of dollars) to the broad, diversified and sophisticated investment possibilities offered by the large, free-market democracies of the US, the EU and Japan. Secondly, according to the IMF[137], at the end of 2008 the financial markets of Africa, the Middle East and Eastern Europe together exceeded just over US$7 trillion (in terms of stock-market capitalisation, debt securities and bank assets) and those of Latin America were just over US$5.4 trillion, whereas total global financial market activity was around US$214.4 trillion. Africa, the Middle East, Eastern Europe and Latin America thus represent just 6% of global financial markets. Furthermore, the United States and other debtor countries are aware of the fact that if creditor countries should threaten to take out their capital, these same financiers would have problems as well. Just think of the possibility of the dollar depreciating and the consequent loss of value of financing countries' foreign currency reserves. The "balance of financial terror", as Larry Summers described today's equilibrium, implies reciprocal interdependence: not only do Western countries need the liquidity of SWFs, as proven by the financial crisis, but SWFs also need Western countries to keep their markets open to foreign investment.

Have Concerns Been Confirmed by Facts?

We have come to a crucial question: does the empirical evidence bear out the concerns cited above? It is important to focus our attention on the actual behaviour of SWFs.

Many of the above concerns have not been confirmed by facts. To date, empirical evidence indicates that SWFs have behaved as economically rational investors who seek to maximise their profits through the proper balancing of risk and return.

Regarding national security, the operations of SWFs have not affected the major OECD countries, nor have they influenced US or EU foreign policy.

Sensitive sectors have not been targeted. As noted in Chapter 4, the technology sector (IT, telecoms and aerospace) amounted to US$17 billion of investment, covering 9% of total recorded transactions by SWFs in the period 1995-July 2009[138], while the defence sector, crucial from the security point of view, only represented 1% with just US$2 billion[139]. This is confirmed by other studies as well. For example, in a 2008 report by Monitor Group[140], out of 785 acquisitions worth US$250 billion made from 2000 to mid-2008, investments in strategic sectors (defence, aerospace, high technology) made up an insignificant percentage (less than 1%) of total investments.

As noted in Chapter 4, the evidence regarding the size of stakes SWFs acquire in companies is mixed. More than half of all transactions involved a 20% stake in the target company (25% involved 100% control)[141]. Miracky and Bortolotti[142] confirm that SWFs take controlling stakes, but specify that this happens mostly in emerging economies while, when they invest in the OECD countries and especially in sensitive sectors, SWFs avoid control. However, the sample databases we refer to include only publicly disclosed transactions and therefore give an incomplete picture. It is rather difficult to identify transactions involving small stakes since they do not require any public disclosure. We must therefore turn to investment policy as declared by the funds. According to the IWG survey[143], 40% of the respondents stated they have limits on the maximum share of ownership that can be held in the same company. According to Truman[144], about half of nonpension SWFs set limits on taking controlling stakes in companies. This percentage rises to 80% for pension funds. For example the largest funds such as ADIA and Norwegian GPF-G are not interested and do not invest in controlling stakes. Moreover, even when large stakes are acquired, SWFs have almost always behaved as passive investors, often acquiring shares without the right to vote, not claiming seats on boards of directors nor intervening in operational decision-making. Only recently, after the financial crisis, has the emphasis on active governance begun to increase. The main exception to this is Norway's GPF-G which has always fully exercised its ownership rights.

Obviously it is possible to pursue political interests without holding controlling shares, even though this is rather difficult. Furthermore, SWFs tend to invest where they find a favourable political climate. This entails the absence of opposition on the part of recipient countries' governments. As Balding[145] has shown, SWFs have a tendency to not stray too far from home and invest in the near abroad. Similarly, Chhaochharia and Laeven[146] find that SWFs tend to invest in countries that share similar cultural traits, showing a preference to invest in the familiar.

In regard to the interests of companies whose shares are held by SWFs, we have not found evidence of SWFs acting counter to them.

However, it cannot be denied that there have been examples of SWFs that have acted on the basis of a political agenda. For example, China's SAFE acquired government bonds from Costa Rica as part of a 2007 agreement under which Costa Rica cut ties with Taiwan[147]. In this case the financial blackmail worked, but between two countries of totally different political and economic size. Norway's pension fund invests on the basis of ethical guidelines, and therefore on the basis of eminently political criteria. It recently divested from a series of companies not in line with these criteria, but according to Beck and Fidora[148] this did not have a significant effect on the prices of the assets involved.

Some SWFs have generated problems with their investments in other countries. One example is Temasek's acquisition of the Shin Corporation in Thailand in 2006. This seems to have contributed to political unrest in that country – which led to the fall of the then-prime minister Thaksin Shinawatra and accelerated the military coup which occurred a few months later.

There are also cases in which SWFs have acted in a strategic fashion. For example, the case in 2008 of CIC, which supposedly financed the state-owned Chinese aluminium company Chinalco through the China Development Bank in order to block, in cooperation with Alcoa (US), the hostile takeover by BHP Billiton (an English mining company) of Rio Tinto (an Australian mining company). The thwarted merger could have created a monopoly, with a consequent rise in the price of iron ore, a crucially important commodity for Chinese industry. This event raised suspicions that SWFs could pursue political targets by interfering with the normal functioning of the private market.

Some studies have recently appeared in academia that for the first time attempt to quantitatively measure the influence of political factors on SWF investment choices and try to understand their economic and political implications. For example, Knill et al[149] examine the causal relationship between SWF investments and political relations by analysing a combined sample of over 900 acquisitions of public and private targets by SWFs during the period 1984-2009. They find evidence that political relations play a role in SWF investment decisions and SWF investment decisions influence political relations. SWFs prefer to invest in nations with which they have relatively weaker political relations and this differentiates them from other economic agents. This could be due to the motivation of investing in order to improve relations with the recipient countries, or to SWF home countries' search for an economic channel for conflict. However, with the information available at the time of writing it was not possible to uncover the full intentions of SWFs and see which one holds true. Moreover the authors found that SWF investment caused a deterioration in political relations with relatively open target countries, while it brought about an improvement when the investment took place in nations that were relatively closed. Although SWF investment decisions may be based on motives that differ from those of other economic actors, the impact of those decisions on political relations appears to be somewhat similar.

In another study, Karolyi and Liao[150] examined the motives and consequences of 5,317 cross-border acquisitions, representing US$619 billion of activity over the period 1990-2008 involving government-controlled buyers. They considered not only SWF-led acquisitions but, more generally, government-led ones. Cross-border acquisition activity involving government-controlled entities over the past 20 years is substantial and growing. The authors found some evidence that government cross-border acquisitions had different features from corporate ones. They tended to target geographically closed countries, were less sensitive to differences in economic development, legal institutions, accounting standards and FDI restrictions and they were more likely to pursue larger targets with greater growth opportunities and more financial constraints. SWF acquisitions differed quite significantly from government-led acquisitions. SWF deals pursued different kinds of targets and the market reactions to their announcements were significantly lower. However, explanatory variables did not lead to the conclusion that governments were markedly different from other economic actors when they invested in financial markets.

According to a recent study by Avendano and Santiso[151], the investment decisions of SWFs do not differ significantly from those of mutual funds, which the authors used as a benchmark of other investors (their sample includes 14,000 holdings for SWFs and 11,600 for mutual funds in the last quarter of 2008). The analysis was made on a geographic and sectoral basis and it showed that there was no significant difference between the two forms of investors' patterns. In addition, when the authors introduced the political variable (i.e. the nature of the political regime in the investing and in the recipient country), they found this variable was not explanatory for SWF investments. The evidence showed that SWFs and mutual funds invest both in democratic and autocratic regimes and that their asset allocations converge. This suggests that SWF investment strategies are financially and not politically driven and therefore their investments are not politically biased.

According to most of the studies examined in Chapter 4, SWFs do not destabilise markets. They have proved to be susceptible to the same market forces as other international investors. Their returns turned negative during the 2007-2009 crisis and their size, in some cases, shrunk. Sovereign wealth funds therefore appear to be rational investors that seek to maximise investment choices through the best risk-return combination. Although the empirical evidence backing up fears expressed up to now cannot be considered conclusive, history has shown that the future is not always a predictable extrapolation of the past. Concerns must be addressed if protectionist closure toward inflows of capital is to be avoided.

Transparency and Good Governance

When there is no transparency, the fears mentioned in the previous section become more pressing: it becomes difficult to understand whether SWFs are pursuing political strategies, and to assess the risks of mismanagement of SWFs themselves and the companies they hold. Therefore, low levels of transparency are likely to strengthen protectionist reactions.

One way to address concerns, founded or unfounded, about SWFs is to promote their transparency[152].

Transparency is important because it is the basis upon which domestic and international stakeholders can ask for explanations behind the investment choices of SWFs.

To date, most SWFs have been reluctant to disclose their investment strategies and performance. It is well known that various governments try to preserve their sovereignty by keeping their financial decisions secret. But when they operate outside national borders, that feature of their sovereignty should not prevail.

Governance is no less important than transparency. Corporate governance is the set of mechanisms used by companies to take and implement decisions and operations, and includes management practices, organisational routines, formal procedures, policies, structures, statutes and decision-making guidelines. Governance norms protect financial institutions from political influence, fraud and corruption, and help maintain accountability and transparency. They ensure that an organisation acts in accordance with its values and within the norms of the society in which it operates[153].

SWFs have been perceived by Western analysts as lacking good governance practices[154]. While in normal Western financial institutions the ultimate stakeholder is an individual, in the case of SWFs the ultimate beneficiary is the government together with the citizenry. In many cases it is unclear to whom SWFs are accountable, or how their internal processes determine investment decisions or their priorities are applied to performance and political interests. Institutional arrangements, such as withdrawal and accumulation rules, investment policies, reporting procedures, and how the fund is integrated into domestic policy frameworks, are in many cases not publicly disclosed.

According to Clark[155], governance must also be seen from the perspective of the home country's citizens' political expectations. The mechanisms of SWF governance in fact must ensure the long-term preservation of wealth and its fair intergenerational distribution. Governance must be solid enough to avoid the temptation of political short-termism and governments spending assets for current political advantage.

Some indices have been devised to measure SWF transparency and governance. We will analyse Edwin Truman's[156] of the Peterson Institute, the most well-known and widely used one, along with the Linaburg-Maduell Transparency Index (LMTI) of the SWF Institute.

Truman's scoreboard covers four fundamental categories:

1. structure

2. governance

3. transparency and accountability

4. behaviour in the market.

Each category contains questions (for a total of 33), most of which are yes/no type, corresponding with 1 and 0 points respectively. Some questions can also be answered with partial points. For each category and for the total, each SWF's score is given by the fund's percentage out of the maximum score. This classification was applied to 44 SWFs. The primary source of evaluation was each fund's regularly and systematically published documents. If these were not available, other public information was used from interviews, websites and press conferences.

The first category, structure, refers to publications and communication regarding goals and strategies, the transparency of financing sources, relations with government budgets and official reserves, and other structural characteristics.

The second category, governance, refers to the separation of government and management roles and the presence of ethical and corporate responsibility guidelines.

The third category of transparency and accountability refers to communicating investment strategies in terms of instruments, benchmarks, use of intermediaries, reporting and its frequency, and auditing and its methods. It entails 14 points, including reporting (on fund size, performance, geographical distribution of investments, details of holdings, and currency composition of portfolio) which carries special weight as it is considered the core of the principle of transparency. In this way funds can be made accountable to the citizens of their home countries, those of recipient countries and in general to market actors. Funds that do not have regular and systematic reporting receive a low rating in this category, and due to its overall importance in Truman's scoreboard they will receive an overall low rating.

The behaviour category refers to the portfolio's management style, assumption of controlling shares, use of leverage, risk management and the use of derivatives.

The funds which have achieved the highest score are New Zealand's Superannuation Fund with 95 points out of 100, followed closely by the Alaska Permanent Fund with 94 points, and the Norwegian Government Pension Fund and the French Fonds de Réserve pour les Retraites (which both scored 92). The SWFs with the worst scores were ADIA of Abu Dhabi, the largest fund, and Qatar Investment Authority, both with only 9 points. In 30 years ADIA has never published any financial information and its lack of transparency is almost legendary. It is all the more problematic due to its size. However ADIA seems to have embraced a more transparent approach and, as has been mentioned, was set to publish for the first time in its history an official report in 2010.

The overall average is higher for the structure category at 75, whereas for governance and transparency average scores are around 50. The worst performance is in the behaviour category with 36 points on average. Overall the distribution of total scores is not excessively skewed: 22 funds had scores over 60, 14 had fewer than 30 points and ten funds were in an intermediate position.

On the basis of Truman's scoreboard, a set of principles were drafted that represented the reference mark for the IWG's task of drawing up a voluntary and shared code of conduct for SWFs, the so-called Santiago Principles analysed in more detail in Chapter 7.

Another transparency index often used is the Linaburg-Maduell Transparency Index (LMTI), named after its two creators, founders as well as vice president and president respectively of the SWF Institute. The index, aimed at measuring transparency, was created based on the conduct of the Norwegian Government Pension Fund, considered the most virtuous example of a SWF in terms of transparency and accountability.

This index is based on ten criteria, each of which can earn a maximum of one point. For the SWF Institute the minimum rating for an adequate level of transparency is eight. Some of the most important points taken into consideration include:

- transparency in terms of origin of wealth and structure of ownership relations

- communication of investment strategies, goals and policies

- publishing periodic reports on shareholdings, geographic distribution and performance of investments

- disclosure of portfolio value

- the existence and modality of an auditing process.

LMTI ranks as the best eight funds (with the maximum score of ten): the Norwegian GPF-G, Temasek, Alaska Permanent Fund, Ireland Pension Fund, Mubadala, Chile Social Stabilization Fund, New Zealand Superannuation Fund, Azerbaijan State Oil Fund. Among the worst performers (with a score of one out of ten): several small funds, plus Algeria Regulation Fund, Brunei Investment Agency, Iran Oil Stabilisation Fund, Nigeria Excess Crude Account, Oman State Reserve Fund and Botswana Pula Fund.

LMTI is not always in line with Truman's scoreboard. For example, in the cases of CIC, Temasek, KIA and Mubadala, scores differ significantly. This can be due to three different reasons. First, LMTI is updated regularly on a quarterly basis on the SWF Institute's website. Therefore it takes into account eventual improvements realised by individual funds; in contrast, Truman's scoreboard was published in 2008, and the 2009 edition, at the time of writing, had yet to be issued. The second reason is that, while LMTI is based on an assessment of a series of desirable variables, Truman's scoreboard is based on comparisons with what other funds actually do. Finally, while Truman's scoreboard includes elements referring to both transparency and governance, LMTI only refers to transparency.

Table 3 contains Truman's scoreboard for each SWF in 2008 (with the details of each of the categories and the total) along with Linaburg-Maduell's updated at third-quarter 2009.

Table 3 – Sovereign wealth funds by asset size, with transparency indices.
Notes are expanded under *Notes on table*, on p.146. Table runs from pp.142-145.

Country	Name of the SWF	T-Str[1]	T-Gov[2]	T-AT[3]	T-Beh[4]	T-Tot[5]	LMTI[6]
UAE	Abu Dhabi Investment Authority (ADIA)	25	0	4	8	9	3
Norway	Norwegian Government Pension Fund – Global	94	100	100	67	92	10
Saudi Arabia	Various funds belonging to Saudi Arabian Monetary Agency (SAMA)	-	-	-	-	-	4
China	SAFE Investment Company	-	-	-	-	-	2
China	China Investment Corporation	50	50	14	17	29	7
Singapore	Government Investment Corporation (GIC)	63	40	39	17	41	6

Country	Name of the SWF	T-Str[1]	T-Gov[2]	T-AT[3]	T-Beh[4]	T-Tot[5]	LMTI[6]
Kuwait	Kuwait Investment Authority (KIA)	75	80	41	0	48	6
China-Hong Kong	Hong Kong Monetary Authority - Investment Portfolio	88	40	79	33	67	8
Singapore	Temasek Holdings	50	50	61	0	45	10
China	National Social Security Fund	100	40	82	67	77	5
Russia	National Wealth Fund	72	40	50	33	51	5
Russia	Reserve Fund	72	40	50	33	51	5
Libya	Libyan Investment Authority	-	-	-	-	-	2
Qatar	Qatar Investment Authority (QIA)	34	0	2	0	9	5
Australia	Australian Government Future Fund (AGFF)	100	80	68	83	80	9
UAE	Investment Corporation of Dubai	-	-	-	-	-	4
Algeria	Revenue Regulation Fund	56	40	11	17	27	1
France	Fonds de Réserve pour les Retraites	100	100	89	83	92	-
USA	Alaska Permanent Fund Corporation (APRF)	100	80	100	83	94	10
Ireland	National Pensions Reserve Fund (NPRF)	100	100	86	58	86	10
Brunei	Brunei Investment Agency (BIA)	31	0	25	0	18	1

Country	Name of the SWF	T-Str[1]	T-Gov[2]	T-AT[3]	T-Beh[4]	T-Tot[5]	LMTI[6]
Kazakhstan	Kazakhstan National Fund (KNF)	88	60	64	33	64	6
Iran	Oil Stabilisation Fund	50	20	18	0	23	1
South Korea	Korea Investment Corporation (KIC)	75	60	45	25	51	9
Malaysia	Khazanah Nasional Berhad (KNB)	44	50	46	0	38	5
UAE	Mubadala Development Company - Abu Dhabi	44	10	7	0	15	10
Nigeria	Excess Crude Oil Account	50	30	14	17	26	1
Canada	Alberta's Heritage Fund	94	60	79	50	74	9
Bahrain	Mumtalakat Holding Company	-	-	-	-	-	8
UAE	Abu Dhabi - International Petroleum Investment Company	-	-	-	-	-	3
USA	New Mexico State Investment Office Trust Fund	100	50	86	100	86	9
Chile	Economic and Social Stabilization Fund (ESSF)	94	60	82	17	70	10
New Zealand	New Zealand Superranuation Fund	100	100	100	75	95	10
Azerbaijan	State Oil Fund (SOFAZ)	88	60	89	50	77	10
UAE	Istithmar World (Dubai World)	38	10	7	0	14	-
Brazil	Sovereign Fund of Brazil	-	-	-	-	-	N/A
Oman	State General Reserve Fund	50	0	18	0	20	1
Botswana	Pula Fund	69	60	54	33	55	3

Country	Name of the SWF	T-Str[1]	T-Gov[2]	T-AT[3]	T-Beh[4]	T-Tot[5]	LMTI[6]
Saudi Arabia	Sanabil Al-Saudia (Public Investment Fund)	-	-	-	-	-	3
Timor-Leste	Timor-Leste Petroleum Fund	100	40	96	50	80	6
USA	Permanent Wyoming Mineral Trust Fund (PWMTF)	100	90	82	100	91	9
Chile	Pension Reserve Fund[7]	94	60	82	17	70	10
USA	Alabama Trust Fund	-	-	-	-	-	6*
Trinidad and Tobago	Heritage and Stabilization Fund	100	60	46	0	53	5
UAE	RAK Investment Authority	-	-	-	-	-	3*
Venezuela	FEM – Macroeconomic Stabilization Fund	50	0	18	17	23	1
Vietnam	State Capital Investment Corporation (SCIC)	-	-	-	-	-	4
Kiribati	Revenue Equalization Reserve Fund	69	60	7	0	29	1
Indonesia	Government Investment Unit	-	-	-	-	-	N/A
Mauritania	National Fund for Hydrocarbon Reserves	-	-	-	-	-	1
Oman	Oman Investment Fund	-	-	-	-	-	N/A
UAE	Emirates Investment Authority	-	-	-	-	-	2

Notes on table

Source: Truman (2008a) and SWF Institute: www.swfinstitute.org/funds.php

* LMTI refers to second quarter 2009 instead of third-quarter 2009.

[1] Truman scoreboard category: structure

[2] Truman scoreboard category: governance

[3] Truman scoreboard category: accountability and transparency

[4] Truman scoreboard category: behaviour

[5] Truman scoreboard: total

[6] Linaburg-Maduell Index updated third-quarter 2009

[7] Same scores as Chile ESSF since ownership, governance and reporting are the same for the two funds.

According to Balding[157], policymakers and scholars focus too much on transparency of SWFs, without considering that in some cases the holding companies of hedge funds and private equity funds are no more transparent than SWFs. Moreover, legal transparency requirements for financial institutions in developed countries did not prevent the spread of the crisis.

The lack or weakness of transparency and good governance are only two of several issues surrounding SWFs. We are aware that voluntary codes of conduct that set best practices for better transparency, accountability and governance cannot definitively address all the questions and concerns that SWFs raise.

In addition, the financial crisis of 2007-2009 demonstrated that even in Western countries the transparency and governance of many financial institutions could not be said to embody best practice. The need to improve governance mechanisms, as well as the transparency of financial information and activities, must therefore be addressed in the proper international fora. This should be on the basis of a comprehensive approach, including all diversified global players interacting in the financial markets. Applying double standards would be damaging. What is requested of SWFs should also be asked of other financial players.

The correlation between transparency and democracy

According to some studies, there is a positive correlation between a fund's level of transparency measured by the Truman index and the level of democracy in a fund's home country. This correlation is shown in Beck and Fidora[158], in Setser[159], in Bertoni[160] as well as in Aizenman and Glick[161].

In Beck and Fidora's paper, Truman's index was correlated with two institutional indicators: an index of the quality of legal systems and an index of countries' levels of democracy (taken from the International Country Risk Guide). The result is a systematic correlation between a low level of transparency, on the one hand, and the low quality of a country's legal system and low levels of democratic accountability, on the other. It is therefore not surprising that SWFs headquartered in OECD countries are more transparent than those in emerging markets, especially in non-democratic countries.

Figure 14 – Transparency and democracy

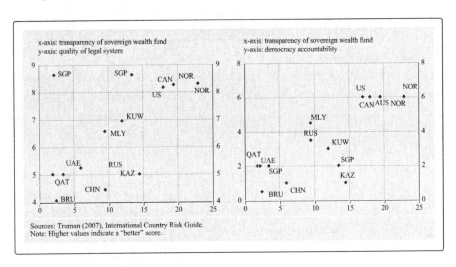

Source: Beck and Fidora (2008).

Setser's testimony and Bertoni's study arrive at the same conclusions by measuring the correlation, which turns out to be positive, between Truman's index and the level of democracy in home countries according to *The Economist* Intelligence Unit's index of democracy.

Figure 15 – Level of transparency (Truman scoreboard) and form of government (*The Economist* index of democracy)

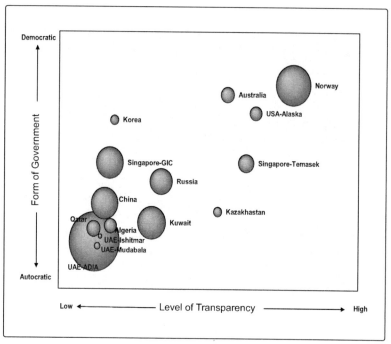

Source: Setser (2008b).

Aizenman and Glick look for a positive correlation between the Truman index and the governance indicators constructed by Kaufmann, Kraay and Mastruzzi[162] (KKM) on the Worldwide Governance Indicators (WGI) of the World Bank. They do not find an obvious correlation between the two. However, when considering not the total average of the KKM index but the sub-index 'Voice and Accountability', which measures the extent to which a country's residents participate in selecting their government and enjoy freedom of expression, the situation changes. This sub-index captures the level of development of democratic institutions and it shows a stronger correlation with Truman's total score. In addition they find that countries with more democratic political institutions are less likely to have SWFs, and those with less democratic political institutions are more likely to have them.

Figure 16 – Transparency and development of democratic institutions (KKM – Voice and Accountability)

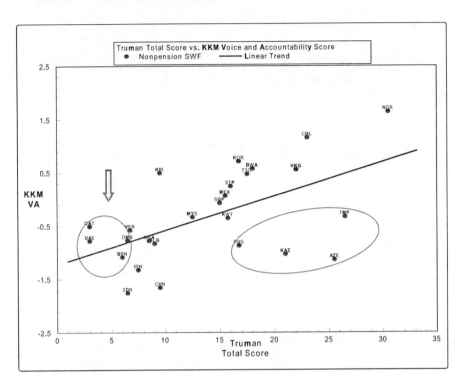

Source: Aizenmann and Glick (2008).

Lyons[163] clusters SWFs into four groups on the basis of the association between the level of transparency (from low to high) and the type of investment approach, whether it be conventional (based on normal portfolio allocation criteria) or strategic. The bottom right group poses little concern as it is transparent and non-strategic. The group in the top left quadrant is more problematic since its SWFs are not transparent and strategic (CIC is included in this group but it has recently improved its level of transparency). The least transparent SWFs are in the bottom left quadrant of the chart (where almost all the Middle Eastern funds are located) and even if they invest in a conventional fashion their opacity raises some concern.

Figure 17 – Transparency and investment approach of SWFs

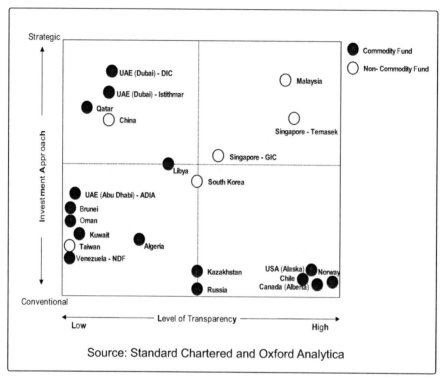

Source: Standard Chartered and Oxford Analytica

Source: Lyons (2007).

The results presented in this paragraph add to concerns over the possibility of SWFs pursuing political-strategic goals, since most funds come from non-democratic countries: these funds' low level of transparency combined with low levels of democracy make the pursuit of non-economic/financial goals more plausible.

Transparency for whom? The point of view of SWF home countries

In this section we take a different perspective – the perspective of the citizens of the countries owning SWFs. Usually the issue of transparency is debated from Western countries' viewpoint, while the interests of the citizens of countries owning SWFs are hardly voiced. Nevertheless we believe that this brief survey on transparency and good governance would not be complete if home countries' points of view were not taken into account.

In democracies too large of a gap between the held portfolio and an optimal portfolio based on the majority of citizens' preferences is unsustainable. Under an authoritarian government, however, the likelihood of accumulating huge surpluses without having to justify such decisions to its own citizens, is much greater. This is not to say that non-democratic regimes do not have to deal with internal constraints. These governments are also confronted with internal dissent, pressure from interest groups and factions within the ruling party apparatus. In China the government received considerable criticism on how the central bank dealt with reserves, as well as investments undertaken abroad by CIC, including Blackstone, especially in 2008 when that firm's stock value dropped by 40%. In Russia the government was criticised for having purchased US$100 billion in Fannie Mae and Freddie Mac securities. In many authoritarian countries extensive criticism of SWFs emerged due to the losses they accumulated during the 2007-2009 crisis, especially for their investment in Western financial institutions. In the Arab world criticism mounted for the way SWFs invested oil windfalls and this caused an increase in the quest for transparency and accountability by civil society and media.

Many SWFs today simultaneously face two types of criticism:

1.   external: the fear that their emerging financial power threatens the West

2.   domestic: the accusation that they waste national surpluses.

The issue essentially concerns the way surpluses must be invested in order to best contribute to a viable economic future for investing nations. Until the crisis, SWFs had attracted more attention in recipient Western countries than in foreign investing countries. Following the crisis the debate gained momentum in investing countries over the ability of SWFs to conserve sovereign wealth. Excess concentration of investment in the financial sector was criticised for the risks it involved and the magnitude of the losses it generated.

In the Arab world, the total lack of scrutiny and accountability fed the suspicion that public finances were imprudently managed and that the blurring of borders between public and private wealth had contributed to investment decisions that were economically unsound but politically motivated by authoritarian regimes' desire to buy foreign powers' support. The plea mounted to give citizens a greater say in how their natural resources wealth was used. The idea of rescuing foreign companies when domestic ones needed support enjoyed little domestic approval and caused many SWFs to reorient themselves toward domestic or regional investment. The comparison between the stunning losses accumulated during the crisis and unemployment and poverty levels in many countries in the region shocked Arab public opinion. The question arose: why were SWFs available to rescue Western banks but not to invest strategically at home and abroad?

As several commentators suggest (see for instance Berehndt)[164] Arab wealth should be invested taking into account the long-term development strategies of their own economies, their diversification and the need for knowledge and technology transfer. SWF resources should also be invested in agriculture, food processing, the water sector, education, health care and renewable energy, all strategic sectors for the region. The final goal should be not only the maximisation of returns, but also and more importantly that wealth is managed in a way that is consistent with long-term interests of the citizenry. The objection usually raised against the suggestion to invest domestically is that oil-rich economies are too small to absorb these huge capital inflows, while oil-poor neighbours are considered not mature enough to absorb them. The 2007-2009 crisis, however, demonstrated that money was not safe if invested in Western institutions either. Even if SWFs are owned by a small portion of Arab oil-rich countries, according to some voices all the region should benefit from the windfall of oil resources – since the conditions of oil-poor countries are strictly associated with the development of the rich ones.

SWFs must be part of a broader project of furthering the economic and political development of the Arab world. As Khouri puts it: "This is a moment when Arabs should be thinking more in terms of enhancing the wealth of their sovereignty, rather than merely bemoaning the erratic performance of their sovereign wealth"[165]. He suggests more constitutional and parliamentary controls over the use of public finance, along with the establishment of councils of surveillance made up by civil society, academia, the private sector and the media. According to him, public finance cannot remain a monarchical or presidential protected domain away from the scrutiny of public opinion.

In this landscape, Islamic finance, according to some commentators in the Islamic world, represents a possible solution to best protect society from the dangers of secular finance. This is why Middle Eastern SWFs are faced with rising pressure from some domestic quarters to increase the percentage of their assets invested in instruments compliant with Islamic finance.

As this is a very complex area which entails not only economic and financial, but also political considerations, it is quite difficult to understand whether SWFs have been beneficial for their own citizens. This is especially difficult on an overall basis, while it is more feasible on a case-by-case approach. An attempt in this direction has been made by Blackburn et al[166], who tried to define a methodology for determining whether SWFs best serve the interests of their own citizens. They have assessed and evaluated potential benefits and costs of SWFs on a case-by-case basis from the point of view of the citizens of the SWF owner countries. Benefits have been compared to possible alternative uses of funds such as lowering taxes or more investment in infrastructure. The potential benefits the authors identify are the ability of SWFs to earn higher risk-adjusted returns than other investments. In addition, they consider non-financial benefits, for example the political leverage and soft power a government can exercise on other countries and companies through SWFs on behalf of its citizens. Costs include the risk that governments perform poorly in picking winners, as well as the protectionist reactions in recipient countries which can add to the costs of using such funds. They focus on costs/benefits provided to citizens by six large funds: ADIA, Norwegian GPF-G, GIC, CIC, KIA, and the Russian former Stabilization Fund. The analysis is complicated by the opacity of some of the funds and the difficulty of assessing returns on political objectives. Based on their methodology, the authors conclude that only Singapore's and Kuwait's funds provide an overall net benefit to their citizens, while for the others, costs exceed benefits and fiscal or external surpluses could be used more efficiently in other ways.

We are aware that additional efforts must be made to analyse financial, economic and political considerations in order to be able to assess the costs and benefits of SWFs for their home citizens. However, the plea is mounting for SWFs to transform themselves into sovereign development funds that allocate an increasing share of their portfolio to responsible investments in real assets in domestic or regional economies.

6.

The United States and the European Union Confronted with SWFs

As a consequence of the concerns outlined above, many states have proceeded to react correctively or preventively. Between 2007 and 2008 at least 11 states, which together represented 40% of all foreign investment inflows in 2006, approved or began drafting laws to restrict foreign direct investment (FDI) and broaden their government's scope for supervising and authorising FDI[167]. Most of these measures were legitimised by the need to defend national security or preserve what were considered strategic sectors.

Every government has always had not only the right, but also the responsibility, to protect its own security in critical sectors, including defence and armaments. The recent novelty is that governments have begun to lengthen the list of sectors to monitor – including unspecified sensitive infrastructure (the United States, France, Germany and Japan); the energy sector (the United States, Russia, and Hungary); cryptology (Russia, Germany, France and Japan); and even gambling (France). In sum, in 2006 the United Nations Conference on Trade and Development (UNCTAD) recorded the highest ever number of restrictive measures. This represented a reversal compared with the previous decade. In the '90s, policy changes were in most cases favourable to FDI. This continued to at least 2001. As a consequence, FDI global inflows continuously increased from 1993, with a halt in 2001, and then started growing again from 2003 through 2007[168].

The reason for the latter trend reversal is not so much the growth of FDI in those years, and particularly FDI coming from emerging markets, but more the fact that the share of that investment ascribable to government entities had grown. SWFs indeed were only part of a larger landscape of sovereign investors that included state-owned enterprises, public pension funds and all those entities ultimately controlled by governments (for example, Russian conglomerates, Chinese government-linked companies, and the private wealth of the Gulf states' ruling families).

In this chapter we will deal with the events that raised concerns in the US and the main EU countries, and then analyse their reactions in regulatory terms. The open question is whether a coherent regulatory framework can be conceived which protects countries' national security and strategic interests but does not discourage inflows of FDI including that of SWFs.

The United States: From Concern to Reaction

The issue of protecting national security vis-à-vis FDI has a long history in the United States, a democracy with strongly patriotic and strategic concerns.

In 1950 the Defence Production Act (DPA) was enacted in response to the Korean War and in defence of national security. Section 721 of this act dealt with regulating FDI. The DPA is still in force, although it has been amended several times. In 1975 the Committee on Foreign Investment in the United States (CFIUS[169]) was established to implement Section 721 of the DPA. CFIUS, subordinate to the Treasury Department, was created to assess the impact of foreign investment on US national security. In 1988, in response to growing concerns about Japanese investment, Congress approved the Exon-Florio Amendment to the DPA, which gave the US president the authority to block acquisitions by foreign entities which jeopardise national security.

At the beginning of the first decade of the 21st century there were various controversial acquisition attempts by sovereign investors which failed. In 2005 Unocal, the ninth-largest US oil company, was about to be acquired by the China National Offshore Oil Corporation (CNOOC), run by the Chinese government. Opposition in the US Senate blocked the operation, the Chinese offer was withdrawn and Unocal was acquired by Chevron.

Another failed acquisition attempt in 2006 involved the Peninsular and Oriental Steam Navigation Company (P&O), which ran several US ports, including in New York and New Jersey. Dubai Ports World, owned by the UAE government (Dubai emirate), obtained approval from the CFIUS for the acquisition, generating serious controversy. Opposition from congress to the fact that strategic infrastructure could end up under the control of a Middle-Eastern country caused Dubai Ports to resell the ports to a US buyer.

These events sharpened the debate in the US over how to protect the country's security and strategic interests from investors from non-democratic, non-transparent governments, suspected of pursuing politico-strategic as opposed to financial objectives.

In June 2007 the Treasury Department published its bi-annual report on International Economic and Exchange Rate Policies[170], which included for the first time an appendix on SWFs[171]. Meanwhile there were multiple laws proposed in congress and the senate aimed at impeding SWF investments in certain sectors or at reforming the process of assessing SWF investments based on the 1988 Exon-Florio Act.

The law, enacted after almost 18 months of debate and signed by the President in July 2007, entered into force in October. The Foreign Investment and National Security Act (FINSA), substituted the previous Exon-Florio amendment and updated the CFIUS's competencies. In April 2008 the CFIUS proposed the final set of executive regulations, which were then issued by the Treasury Department in November 2008.

FINSA confirmed and reinforced the CFIUS's focus on protecting national security. The CFIUS had the option to start a review process in case a foreign investor obtained control of a US company by merger, acquisition or takeover, thus putting national security at risk.

Regarding the definition of *control* of a company, the CFIUS regulations did not specify an exact threshold but defined control as any situation in which significant decision-making power could directly or indirectly be exercised. For this reason, even acquisitions of less than 10% could be considered controlling as long as they were not unequivocally passive investments.

Reviewed transactions turn into a more thorough investigation if they are deemed to be potentially detrimental to national security. According to the changes introduced by FINSA, the transformation of the review into investigation is mandatory when the investor is state-owned (SWFs fall into this category), or if the foreign investor gains control of critical infrastructure. The latter is not defined *a priori* in the executive regulations, leaving space for case-by-case assessment.

If at the end of the investigation the transaction is judged innocuous by the CFIUS, it may no longer be contested on the basis of national security motivations. If CFIUS ascertains a risk for national security, FINSA grants it the authority to:

- take measures to correct transactions in order to mitigate the risk (for example suspending voting rights)

- monitor their implementation

- reopen the procedure or apply sanctions if omissions have been ascertained or documentation is considered false or misleading, or if one of the parties has intentionally violated agreements

- request that the president decide whether to suspend or block the operation if measures to mitigate the risk are considered not sufficient to balance the threat to national security.

This entire process may not last longer than three months: one month for the review phase, 45 days for the investigation and a maximum of 15 days for the president's decision, if requested.

FINSA has increased Congress's supervision of the CFIUS by requesting written reports of each investigation and an annual report on its activities, under oath of confidentiality. FINSA has also significantly enhanced the CFIUS's role by improving its transparency and predictability. The organisations representing the major foreign investors in the US favourably accepted the new regulations, since on the one hand they contributed to lessening the climate of hostility surrounding FDI, and on the other they brought greater clarity in terms of timing and criteria for receiving investment.

However, FINSA has also made the process of reviewing foreign investments more complicated, and the US is now one of the most demanding of OECD countries. This could discourage investors, including SWFs, due to the greater cost in terms of time and money. Since inward FDI flows in the US have continued to grow (from 2005 to 2008 they increased from US$105 billion to US$316 billion[172]), it is difficult to determine how this more intense scrutiny may have slowed inflows.

The number of transactions handled by the CFIUS went from 64 in 2005 to 138 in 2007 and 155 in 2008. Similarly, the number of transactions requiring a second level of investigation grew from just one in 2005 to 23 in 2008. From 1997 – when CFIUS first negotiated a mitigation measure – through 2008, CFIUS entered into a total of 51 mitigation agreements. Fourteen of those were undertaken in 2007, while only two were in 2008. In the period 2005-2008 only two presidential decisions were taken, both in 2006[173].

In addition to this system of auditing/authorisation specifically concerning the issue of national security, there are other laws and regulations investors in the US are subject to (for example, disclosure requirements for participations of more than 5% in a company, anti-corruption laws, industry specific regulations), but it is beyond the scope of this work to go deeper into the details of the US's broader investment legislation.

The overall framework that regulates foreign investments in the US appears to be efficient in the sense that it is difficult for transactions that put national security at risk to avoid the scrutiny of the regulatory bodies.

However, diverse opinions circulate on the matter. According to some commentators, in spite of the framework outlined here, the scope for legislation in the US for the specific case of SWF investments can be broadened. For example, Gilson and Milhaupt[174] propose that voting rights of SWFs be frozen until they are transferred to non-state owners. The intended result would be to drive away those SWFs with supposed strategic-political motivations, whilst retaining purely financially-motivated investments. However, instead of being "minimalist" as the authors define it, in our opinion this proposal would more likely risk driving away SFWs from the US and triggering retaliation abroad towards American investors. Countries are rarely insensitive to such snubs. Others[175] propose rules such as forcing SWFs to invest through third-party asset managers. This would be an alternative to requiring them to disclose their shareholder voting records if shareholdings are above a certain size.

Some see a protectionist drift in these proposals for increased regulation of SWFs, arguing that any additional requirements placed on SWF investment would result in an excessive burden and could drive away several billion dollars from the US[176]. So far SWFs have acted like normal investors, and the risk of their acting strategically in the future is significantly limited by existing regulation. After all, American liberalism towards FDI and SWFs has not been disarmed.

European Countries: a Variety of Options

The EU has recently undergone an upswing in SWF investment. It clearly shows these investors' significant interest in the continent. The EU may not erect barriers to foreign investment without violating its numerous internal and international obligations: internal obligations in the sense that economic openness is a cornerstone of the single market and European integration; international obligations in terms of all the agreements signed with international institutions such as the IMF, the OECD, the World Trade Organisation (WTO) and various bilateral treaties with other regional blocs or single countries. Extricating itself from this host of EU and international obligations is not easy.

As for internal obligations, the free movement of capital is one of the pillars of the single market. Article 63 TFEU (Treaty on the Functioning of the EU) (ex Art. 56 TEC) establishes the principle of free movement of capital within the single market and prohibits all restrictions not only between member states, but also between member states and third countries. This markedly laissez-faire approach is tempered by the following articles of the TFEU: 64 (ex Art. 57 TEC), 65 (ex Art. 58 TEC), 66 (ex Art. 59 TEC) and 75 (ex Art. 60 TEC) which allow for exceptions, on an EU and national level, to the principle of free movement, always interpreted restrictively by the European Court's jurisprudence.

Based on the exceptions provided for by the TFEU, most countries do have laws that restrict foreign investment for reasons of national security, and which give national governments the right to review proposed investments. If member states exercise their discretionary power to block investments for reasons other than the exceptions provided for by the TFEU, this would lead to legal action by the European Commission and possibly the Court of Justice. Member states' measures moreover must notably obey the principle of proportionality as defined by the Court. This existing regulatory framework provides a comprehensive regime for regulating investment from any foreign investor including SWFs.

We will now look at the regulatory approaches and reactions of the major European countries (Germany, France, the United Kingdom and Italy), which have the four highest GDPs among the EU27 Members[177]. We will focus on the specific issue of protecting national security. The European situation is rather fragmented and this does not help the single market or European companies, both of whom risk losing long-term potential investors with enormous liquidity. We will then analyse the European Commission's approach, together with the proposals put forward by several commentators to cope with the rise of SWFs.

Germany

In 2007, the attempt by the Russian Mischkonzerns Sistema to acquire a share of Deutsche Telekom, and that of the Russian bank Vneshtorgbank to acquire shares in EADS, a European leader in aerospace and defence, created a climate of distrust towards foreign investors controlled by governments. In April 2008, the German government, increasingly concerned about SWF and state-owned company (SOE) investments – in particular Russian ones, and especially in the energy sector – announced its intention to issue new legislation authorising the Ministry of Economics and Technology to subject foreign investments from state-owned entities to an approval process. This also meant investments by SWFs. In the summer of 2008 one event accelerated the government's decision in particular: the attempt by Neptune Orient Lines, controlled by Temasek Holdings, Singapore's SWF, to acquire Hapag-Lloyd, a major maritime transport company based in Hamburg. The acquisition did not come through due to opposition by the German government and public opinion. The Hamburg-based company was then bought by a group of local investors.

In August 2008, the Federal Government proposed an amendment to the Foreign Trade and Payments Act passed in 1961 for verifying foreign investment in the defence sector. In April 2009 this amendment and its implementing ordinance came into force[178]. According to the amendment, any investment in a quoted or non-quoted German company in which a foreign investor from outside the EU or European Free Trade Association (EFTA) obtains over 25% ownership may be subject to formal investigation by the Federal Ministry of Economics and Technology. The law also applies to cases in which 25% is not obtained directly, but by agreements with third parties on exercising the right to vote. The purpose of the authorisation process is to assess the impact of transactions on national security and public order. The problem is that the proposal creates significant ambiguity in terms of the meaning of national security as well as applicable sectors, which are not specified.

Investigation is undertaken by the Federal Ministry of Economics and Technology, which has three months to decide whether the transaction could damage national security or public order. If the response is that it could, the minister notifies the buyer that further investigation will be carried out. Starting from this notification, the ministry has two months to block the transaction with the approval of the Federal Government, or to accept it with reservations, i.e. imposing certain conditions. Otherwise the transaction is considered accepted. The amendment also provides for investigation by the Federal Ministry if the investors are based inside the EU and EFTA on the condition that a non-EU or non-EFTA owner holds at least 25% of the acquirer's voting rights and that there is an indication of an abusive situation attempting to circumvent the spirit of the law.

This law is very similar to the American FINSA; however, the 25% limit makes it seemingly one of the less restrictive laws internationally. In spite of this, the proposal met a series of negative reactions and was accused by many of being protectionist and damaging for Germany's image as a liberal country, open to foreign investment. The Federation of German Industries expressed concern about the law. Despite the ameliorations made during the legislative process, in our opinion some serious weaknesses remain. For example, the fact that the maximum length of time required for the process is five months: three months to decide whether to start an investigation, and two to complete the investigation itself. This extensive waiting period raises investors' costs and uncertainty, possibly causing them to look elsewhere to invest (the US, for example, where the process is shorter).

Overall, it is difficult to judge this approach *a priori*. Much depends on how it will be applied, since the concepts of public order and national security leave ample room for discretion. The Federal Government ensures the law will be rarely and narrowly applied. Doubts remain as to whether the amendment is in line with EU law or contravenes the free movement of capital within the EU.

France

The French government issued a decree governing foreign investment in December 2005 (Decree No. 2005 – 1739) which updated the article L 151-3 (2004) of the Code Monétaire et Financier.

This decree provides for a process of authorisation – conducted by the Ministry of Economy, Industry and Employment – for foreign investors, both EU and non-EU, to acquire companies in 11 sectors considered sensitive for national interests (including gambling!). However, the decree differentiates between EU and non-EU investors in that the scope of the authorisation procedure is broader for investments originating from third countries. The declared objective is to protect public order, public safety and national defence. Investigation is undertaken when the transaction involves:

- the takeover of a company operating in France

- the direct or indirect acquisition of a branch of a French company

- foreign investors' direct or indirect acquisition of control of more than one-third of the holdings or voting rights of a company with legal headquarters in France in the specified sectors.

The Ministry of Economy, Industry and Employment is responsible for the process of investigation and notifying the buyer. The ministry can decide to approve the transaction, reject it or approve it under certain conditions to mitigate any perceived risks. The process takes 60 days from the date documentation is delivered, but additional extensions are possible. The French government has not yet officially blocked any transactions.

France received a letter of formal notice, the first stage of the infringement procedure (under Art 258 TFEU ex Art. 226 TEC), in 2006 from the European Commission on this decree because it is considered in breach of Art 63 TFEU (ex Art. 56 TEC) on the free movement of capital and of Art. 49 TFEU (ex Art 43 TEC) on the right of establishment. After the formal French reply, in early 2010 the Commission still had not formally brought the matter before the Court of Justice.

The broader French approach to SWFs is quite complex and nuanced. Positions have varied over time between protectionism and openness conditional only on reciprocity.

In May 2008 the government's finance inspector Alain Demarolle responded to the solicitation by the French Ministry of Economy, Industry and Employment to deal with the subject of SWFs and issued a report on them[179]. This report showed a certain openness to SWF investments. After recognising the increasing financial weight of SWFs, Demarolle recalled the insufficiency of French national savings alone, especially in equities, for the future growth of the French economy; and pointed to the economy's need for long-term foreign investors. SWFs were invited to invest in French companies that represented industrial excellence in important and established sectors. Promising sectors such as renewable energy and SMEs were also suggested as interesting investment opportunities for SWFs. Their investments would be facilitated through a regime of control that was clear and less restrictive than in other countries, and featured the absence of any discrimination against SWFs. The strategy outlined by Demarolle in his report was based on three pillars: establishing a dialogue with SWFs; creating links between SWFs and French companies; recognising the principle of reciprocity. On a European level, France wanted to act in order to align the interests of EU host countries with SWFs, through a comprehensive European approach based on the principles of non-discrimination and reciprocity.

However, the Demarolle report did not prevent steps toward a more protectionist approach in France, as indicated by the French government's decision to establish its own SWF in November 2008. The fund, called the Strategic Investment Fund (SIF), invests in shareholdings in small and medium-sized enterprises and in the capital of large strategic French corporations to protect them from hostile foreign acquisitions. With a founding capital of €20 billion from the Caisse des Dépôts et Consignations (CDC) and the French government, the fund is legally a subsidiary of the CDC and is under its supervision. Its mandate is to act in the public interest, with a long-term view. Its formation does not correspond to the definition of a SWF as provided in Chapter 2, since it has an exclusively domestic focus.

During his term as EU President, Nicolas Sarkozy tried to press the EU to take the same approach, pushing in the second half of 2008 for the establishment of a European sovereign fund[180], a proposal also endorsed by the Italian Minister of Economy and Finance, Giulio Tremonti.

The French strategy has thus been in something of a continuous evolution. From protectionist positions characterised by a tendency to intervene even outside a formal process, to a strategic approach in which, probably as a consequence of the crisis, the final purpose appears twofold: to secure long-term financial resources for the French economy and, at the same time, to attain a level of increased openness amongst SWF home countries towards French companies investing abroad.

United Kingdom

This is the EU country most open to FDI and one of the most open in the world due to its marked laissez-faire attitude and the prevalence of the so-called 'Wimbledon effect', according to which, regardless of players' nationalities, what counts is to host the tournament.

The main purpose of Great Britain's 2002 Enterprise Act was to review mergers and acquisitions to protect market competition. However, among its many provisions, the Act also gave the government the right to block or restrict foreign acquisitions if they went against the public interest in the field of national security.

As far as SWFs are specifically concerned, the UK aspires to make London their global hub. Indeed the UK's friendship with SWFs dates back to the beginning of this story, the year 1953, when the newly created Kuwait Investment Board established its office in London. Factors contributing to the UK's allure for SWFs include traditional

British economic openness towards foreign investors; huge, liquid, scarcely volatile markets; and a predictable regulatory environment unaffected by the latest wave of national concern about public security that has prevailed in other countries such as the US, France or Germany. It is no wonder that the UK is the preferred investment target of SWFs (particularly those from the Middle East) in Europe and one of the most preferred in the world. Between 2006 and 2008, half of all the investments by Middle Eastern funds went to the UK[181]. As already noted in Chapter 4, the UK receives about half of the total invested in the EU by all SWFs, while the second country – Germany, with 15% – lies far behind[182].

Even during the 2007-2009 crisis, London preserved its role as the leading global financial services hub in Europe. The British government gladly accepted and encouraged SWF investment in its financial sector, seriously hit by the crisis.

In spite of its laissez-faire attitude, the UK has endorsed demands for greater transparency and regulation of SWFs. It supports the IMF's initiative in this direction.

Italy

While it does not have Britain's distinct laissez-faire approach, Italy is classified by the OECD as one of the European countries most open to FDI in terms of legislation.

However, an attempt was made in 2001 to issue restrictive regulatory measures toward foreign investors, with the purpose of preserving strategic sectors. Legislative Decree no. 192 froze voting rights for shareholdings of over 2% in companies operating in the electricity and natural gas sectors, should these holdings be acquired by foreign-held companies. The European Commission reacted immediately, formally opposing the Italian government. In 2004 the matter went to trial before the European Court of Justice, which concluded by condemning Italy for violating the principle of free movement of capital (Art. 63 TFEU ex Art. 56 TEC).

In the fall of 2008, the possibility of introducing a 5% limit on SWF holdings in Italian companies was discussed. This followed on from the

Libyan SWF's recent acquisition of 4.9% of UniCredit. The proposal, however, provoked a negative reaction, especially amongst economic operators, and did not become law. Indeed, the Italian government's attitude changed significantly after that, instead focusing on attracting capital from funds considered 'friends'. To this end the Italian government also established a Strategic Committee to promote national interests in dealing with SWFs intending to invest in Italy.

In the end, neither the investment in UniCredit by LIA nor that in ENI made by the same fund – both acquisitions in strategic companies – triggered legislation. Neither did these acquisitions cause concern among public opinion. This reveals, for all the controversy of its 2001 actions, a very open attitude on the part of Italy.

The European Commission's Approach

In spite of its member countries' activism and concern, the EU has not implemented a set of new common regulations regarding SWFs. The European Commission considers the existing legal framework regulating foreign investments (including SWFs) capable of guaranteeing the proper balance between the principle of free movement of capital and legitimate national interests in preserving public security and safety.

However, the excess of uncoordinated national regulations runs the risk of interfering with one of the pillars of European construction, the internal market, as well as damaging the ability of European economies to reap the benefits of the long-term investment of SWFs. For this reason, the commission decided in 2008 to define a common European approach to SWFs. This would be based on a cooperative effort between funds and recipient countries to abide by certain principles of transparency and accountability, and on advising member countries to employ existing regulatory instruments without violating European treaties. On 27 February 2008 the European Commission issued memorandum 115/2008, entitled 'A common European approach to Sovereign Wealth Funds'[183]. Since it was a communication it had no legal binding power. But it exercised soft power by inviting European governments to:

- remain open to foreign investment and avoid a protectionist spiral

- support the solutions shared globally, as proposed by the IMF and the OECD

- use existing European and national regulatory instruments

- respect the EU treaties and the EU's international commitments to the free movement of capital

- respect the principles of proportionality and transparency of rules in any reaction to investments by SWFs.

With regards to SWFs, the commission identified two fundamental principles that they should comply with: good governance and effective transparency. Recommended principles of good governance included:

- clear separation of owners' and managers' responsibilities

- clear definition of investment policies and correlated objectives

- public communication of general principles governing the relationship of a SWF with its government, and their principles of internal governance

- the development of risk-management policies.

In terms of transparency, it commended:

- annual publication of investment positions and portfolio activities, especially for controlling stakes

- disclosing criteria for exercising ownership and voting rights

- publication of data on the use of leverage and portfolio currency composition

- publication of a fund's size and financial sources

- communication of the home country's regulations and controls governing the fund.

This memorandum was presented on 4 March 2008 to ECOFIN (Economic and Financial Affairs Council) and approved by the European Council at its spring summit of March 13-14 that same year[184]. The council reiterated the EU's commitment not to adopt measures that could damage the international openness of markets. The council also confirmed its support for the IMF and OECD initiatives, and reaffirmed the duty of member states to act within the limits set out by the commission's communication and ultimately by European treaties themselves.

The European Parliament (EP) also welcomed the commission's announcement. However, at point five of the final text adopted, the EP requested "the Commission to conduct an analysis of tools at the European Union's disposal in EC Treaty provisions and existing legislation – such as transparency requirements, voting rights, shareholders' rights and golden shares – that would allow some reaction in the event of ownership problems due to SWF intervention."[185]

There are significant differences between the commission's position and that of major EU countries (in particular France and Germany). The commission emphasised the importance of the internal market's openness to FDI in order to achieve economic prosperity across the continent. The legislation issued by countries like France and Germany, though, may appear stricter than suggested by European Commission. However, in our opinion, it is not disproportionate; protecting national security in this way is legitimate. Of course it will be up to the European Court of Justice to decide whether this is in line with EU law.

The commission's approach has been endorsed by many[186] who believe that the current EU legal framework – as defined by the Treaty on the Functioning of the European Union, the court's jurisprudence, the soft power exercised by the commission and member states' right of initiative – is the best way to preserve European openness to foreign investment and therefore European economic prosperity.

According to other commentators, however, the commission's memorandum, although it managed to synthesise the 27 member states' heterogeneous positions, did not appear to be an adequate answer. There were several proposals for reaction at the European level.

Some suggested the establishment of a CFIUS-type screening mechanism at EU level to evaluate third countries' investments (including SWFs) in terms of their impact on European security[187]. While this proposal could safeguard the single market, it would be difficult to realise. In fact, the commission does not have the power to settle agreements on direct investments with third countries. And it seems likely to be equally difficult for it to obtain the necessary legitimacy to decide matters of national security. There are, for example, no intelligence services at the community level, and no political or strategic interests common to *all* member countries. So for European institutions in their current form to carry out national security-related economic activity is not a particularly credible option at this stage. The creation of an ad-hoc institution is still less convincing. This approach has, anyway, been clearly rejected by the commission and the council.

There are those who advocated the possible adoption of legislation at EU level that would provide the legal framework, to be implemented at national level, for the review of foreign acquisitions and investment[188]. The EU legislation would define the rules, the maximum duration of the process, the definition of what would be considered control, the list of the sectors where this would be relevant, and a framework for negotiating mitigation agreements. If one of the members was found to breach those rules, it would then be possible to bring the matter before the Court of Justice. This solution would avoid confusion and a lack of coordination amongst national regimes.

According to others[189], it would be advisable to apply a principle of reciprocity vis-à-vis third countries that wanted to invest in Europe. Why should Europe keep its markets open to third parties when these countries are nearly inaccessible? The problem was that reciprocity is difficult to implement concretely, and risks leading to a spiral of closure rather than openness – especially given that many SWF owners are emerging countries that cannot be forced to suddenly comply with recipient countries' standards. Besides, the OECD recommends that its members set aside the principle of reciprocity in regulating capital movement.

Finally, some proposed the establishment of a European SWF. This proposal, of French and Italian origin, appears the most convincing to us. We will address it in the next section.

Another initiative undertaken at EU level may seem rather similar to the idea of a European SWF, although significant differences exist that will be clarified in a moment. In 2009 the French Caisse des Dépôts et Consignations (CDC) together with the Italian Cassa Depositi e Prestiti (CDP), the German Kreditanstalt für Wiederaufbau (KfW) and the European Investment Bank (EIB) established the Club of Long-Term Investors. Its purpose is to promote coordinated action at the European level for raising new long-term financing instruments for energy and infrastructure projects[190]. Club members share the view that the crisis was primarily due to the short-termism of financial market operators. They aim to promote economic and financial stability in the post-crisis world and to finance long-term projects of public interest. The actors involved share characteristics similar to SWFs (such as long-term horizons and investment strategies, a broader approach to investments than pure profit maximisation, and no liquidity constraints). Indeed SWFs have been invited – and some of them have already accepted – to join the Club. More than a response to the arrival of SWFs, the Club of Long-Term Investors seems to represent the European version, with its own characteristics, strategies and purposes, of a SWF. It has been included in this section in accordance with this broader view.

Beyond the hypothetical proposals mentioned so far, there currently seems to be only two feasible and complementary solutions: the global regulatory response by the IMF to create a code of conduct on a voluntary basis for SWFs; and the efforts of the OECD to define rules of behaviour for recipient countries. These are hopefully the most effective approaches, at least in the medium term, and perfectly in line with the multilateral approach enshrined in the EU tradition. Indeed the European Commission has been actively involved in the work of both the IMF and the OECD.

The proposal for a European sovereign fund

The creation of a European Sovereign Fund (ESF), a bold and innovative European response to SWFs, has already been proposed by the authors of this book[191]. Done properly, in our view this would constitute (and require) a renewal of the economic-institutional engineering capability that the EU demonstrated in its first 50 years of integration.

We propose the creation of a SWF on an EMU (Economic and Monetary Union) level, with a view to broadening the "enhanced cooperation" already in place with the euro and entailed in the EU treaties (art. 20 TEU and art. 326 to 334 TFEU). This SWF could actually compete with other SWFs, and at the same time contribute to the development needs and economic strategies of the eurozone countries. It would be an important complement to a global economic power like the EMU.

The ESF would have as collateral the official gold reserves of EMU countries. As of January 2010 these reserves amounted to 347 million ounces, which at the price of US$1000 an ounce would have a counter value of almost US$350 billion[192]. This would make the ESF one of the largest SWFs in the world. We single out the potential of gold reserves as we believe they will again play a key role in the international monetary and financial system – especially after the 2007-2009 crisis, as China's interest in gold (cf. Chapter 2) seems to confirm.

The new European fund should obviously feature maximum transparency and all proper governance arrangements. It could invest in the euro area by financing companies, banks and domestic infrastructure, as well as in other markets, including emerging ones, focusing on strategic sectors (for example, energy and natural resources).

We know that to create such a fund there would be various issues to clarify and resolve in relation to the Central Bank Gold Agreement (CBGA). Other issues include the statutes of the euro system, determining the legal nature of the ESF, its relationship with the ECB and eventual private shareholders. Not forgetting, too, defining appropriate institutional arrangements so as to optimally balance market criteria with political considerations.

The ESF forms part of a larger project proposed by Quadrio Curzio[193] – to raise €1,000 billion by issuing European debt securities. The Eurobonds originally proposed in 1992 by Jacques Delors should also be guaranteed by the ECB and EMU governments to pay interest not exceeding that of German 10-year bonds, because of their low risk. Voting powers in this extended ESF should be proportionate to the GDP of EMU countries, with consideration of gold reserves conferred and their debt as a percentage of GDP. The financial resources raised should enhance long-term investments in the EU and contribute to financing member states, who would pay interest on the loans received.

The experience of the EU, and the seriousness of the post 2007-2009 financial situation, might be enough to see such a bold move through.

7.

The Principles of the IMF and the OECD: Towards a Multilateral Framework

Developing a Multilateral Framework

Confronted with SWFs and the fictitious or real threats they pose, as noted in the previous chapter national governments have begun to address the phenomenon – and each with their own approach. The main risk of such individual, uncoordinated and sometimes politically-driven reactions is that they could encourage a drift towards protectionism, causing the fragmentation of global financial markets.

Striking the balance between the economic benefits SWFs may provide, and their supposed potential for jeopardising national security, is something that can only be partially carried out at a state level. "The Great Trade-off" as Cohen[194] has called it, or the balance between investment openness and national security, can and should be addressed with a multilateral approach at the international level.

Awareness of this fact was one of the main reasons behind the decisions of the IMF and the OECD to define shared principles for the conduct of SWFs and recipient countries. This was undertaken in order to avoid the excesses both of an unregulated free market and of protectionism.

There are numerous precedents for the IMF's efforts regarding SWFs[195]. They include work in the past by the G8, the US Department of the Treasury, and the European Commission. None, however, approach the comprehensiveness of what resulted in the Santiago Principles.

The International Monetary Fund and the Santiago Principles

In May 2008 the IMF established an international working group (the International Working Group of Sovereign Wealth Funds, IWG) with representatives from 23 governments owning SWFs: Australia, Azerbaijan, Bahrain, Botswana, Canada, Chile, China, Equatorial Guinea, Iran, Ireland, South Korea, Kuwait, Libya, Mexico, New Zealand, Norway, Qatar, Russia, Singapore, East Timor, Trinidad and Tobago, the United Arab Emirates, and the United States. These representatives were joined by some permanent observers: Oman, Saudi Arabia, Vietnam, the OECD and the World Bank. The group also included representatives from recipient countries.

The IWG was co-chaired by Hamad Al Suwaidi, Under Secretary of Finance of Abu Dhabi and Member of the Board of Directors of ADIA, and Jaime Caruana, Director of the IMF's Monetary and Capital Markets Department. The choice not to deal unilaterally with the issues raised by SWFs, but instead to form a group composed of representatives from countries owning SWFs in order to achieve a shared formulation of principles, turned out to be rather effective. The group was able to accommodate heterogeneous actors with divergent and in some cases conflicting political interests and managed to overcome the distrust shown by some members, particularly Russia and China, towards the initiative, successfully creating a climate of cooperation among home countries and recipient countries. The negotiations were concluded in just six months.

The IWG was assigned the task of drawing up a code of conduct for SWFs under the coordination of the IMF. To this end the IWG met three times: in Washington DC, Singapore and Santiago. At the third meeting, on 11 October 2008, the IWG published the 24 guiding principles (Generally Accepted Principles and Practices, GAPP[196]) also called the Santiago Principles for the name of the Chilean capital where they were approved. They are contained in the Appendix of this book.

Compliance is voluntary. The principles should help in creating trust towards SWFs both in home and recipient countries, and thus contribute to maintaining a stable and open international investment climate. These principles are subordinate to national laws and regulations, so their applicability depends on how compatible they are with the laws of each country involved. GAPP covers three broad areas:

1. legal framework, objectives and coordination with macroeconomic policies

2. institutional framework and governance structure

3. investment and risk management.

The first area of the GAPP, points one through five, pertains to the soundness of the legal structure, which should be made public and should be able to achieve established objectives; definition and publication of objectives; coordination of SWF activities with the owner country's monetary and fiscal policies; definition and publication of financing sources, rules for drawing and expenditures; and provision of relevant statistical data for owner countries' macroeconomic statistical purposes.

The second area of the GAPP, points six to 17, defines a framework for governance to ensure clear division of roles and responsibilities and to facilitate the operational independence of management. According to GAPP 10 and 16, this framework should also be properly officialised and publicised.

The optimal attribution of tasks and duties to owners, government bodies and operative management – in order to ensure independence from political interference – is the focus of points seven to nine of the GAPP. GAPP 13 states that the required ethical and professional standards for operating the fund should be publicised. Points 11 and 12 of the GAPP recommend the preparation of an annual report containing information on a fund's operations and results; this should be drawn up and certified according to internationally or nationally recognised accounting standards. More generally, GAPP 17 recommends public disclosure of all financial information pertaining to a fund's economic and financial orientation.

In the same area are two other principles which seem to be heterogeneous compared to the rest of the group. GAPP 14 requests that relationships with third parties for purposes of operational management of the fund be based on economic and financial motivations. GAPP 15 states that operations in host countries should be conducted in compliance with all applicable regulatory and disclosure requirements of the countries in which they operate. This requirement is so obvious that it seems superfluous.

In the third area, points 18 to 24, the principles pertain to defining and publicising funds' investment policies. In addition to being based on solid principles of portfolio management, these should set out a fund's degree of financial-risk exposure, its use of leverage, use of external managers, and its exercise of ownership rights (GAPP 18). GAPP 19 states that the investment goal should be to maximise financial returns. This does not, however, preclude investment decisions being based on motivations other than economic and financial ones, as long as these are clearly disclosed. GAPP 20 requires SWFs not to derive undue advantage from the power of the government to which they belong, when competing with the private sector. GAPP 22 focuses on defining and implementing proper risk-management policies. Finally, GAPP 24 urges each SWF to conduct regular reviews of the implementation of GAPP principles.

These principles are in line with market practices adopted by major international financial institutions and reflect what already occurs in the most transparent SWFs. They are based not only on the recommendations of the main institutions involved, ranging from the US Treasury to the EU Commission, but also on the most authoritative studies conducted on the subject, including Truman's[197].

According to the most optimistic views, if these principles are applied SWFs will improve their transparency, accountability and governance. And this will contribute to greater stability in international financial markets and the greater openness of national markets to foreign investment. Often overlooked is that the citizens in SWF home countries would also benefit from greater transparency, by being better able to evaluate how their national wealth is being utilised.

The GAPP have been criticised somewhat for such unrealistic expectations. They have also been censured for being generic formulations, difficult to verify. In response, the authors have averred that the principles were formulated broadly, after due consideration, so that they could be adapted to different institutional and legal contexts, and to different types of funds. The European Commission commented that more emphasis could have been placed on transparency, requesting more information in terms of shareholdings, currency composition, and the exercise of voting rights. Others perceived a limit to the voluntary adoption of the principles.

It must be acknowledged, however, that a cogent set of regulations drawn up unilaterally is unlikely to have been more effective than voluntary principles drafted collectively. According to other critiques, the code of conduct risked being ineffectual due to the IMF's inability to monitor or impose sanctions. (Most of the countries concerned by the GAPP are not IMF borrowers and therefore are not subject to IMF conditionality.) At the same time, however, most of them *are* intent on increasing their representation at the fund. They were therefore willing to show commitment to the GAPP as a means of visibly contributing to the stability of the international financial system.

It is already a good sign that representatives from the home countries of the world's least transparent and largest SWFs (China, UAE, Kuwait, Qatar and Russia) have taken part in the IWG's work and pledged to comply with the principles (with the exception of Saudi Arabia, which asked to participate as an observer since SAMA does not consider itself a SWF). To incentivise the compliance of further funds, non-compliance will almost certainly have to entail certain consequences – protective as much as punitive– first and foremost increased market closure on the part of recipient economies. The GAPP should also be established as a mark of quality; the strongest incentive to abide by these rules will probably be prestige and reputation.

For all these reasons the Santiago Principles should be seen as more of a starting point than the finish line.

In fact, in 2009 the IWG proposed the formation of a permanent supervisory body for SWFs. It would have the tasks of supervising compliance with the Santiago Principles, updating the GAPP, and facilitating their diffusion, comprehension and implementation. In the next section we will examine the follow-up to this proposal.

The International Forum of Sovereign Wealth Funds (IFSWF)

To address the issue of monitoring and to provide a follow-up to the Santiago initiative, the International Forum of Sovereign Wealth Funds (IFSWF) was established by the IWG at a meeting in Kuwait City in April 2009.

The Kuwait declaration[198] that established the IFSWF defined the purpose, members and structure of the forum. It would be a voluntary group of SWFs, without legal force and with the main purpose of exchanging views on issues of common interest – including SWF activities, risk management, interactions with the financial system, facilitating the understanding and application of the Santiago Principles and encouraging cooperation with recipient countries to promote an open investment environment.

Members who participate in the forum must have taken part in the IWG and endorsed the Santiago Principles. If they have not participated in the IWG, they must still comply with the principles. In 2010 its members were: Australia, Azerbaijan, Bahrain, Botswana, Canada, Chile, China, East Timor, Equatorial Guinea, Iran, Ireland, Korea, Kuwait, Libya, Mexico, New Zealand, Norway, Qatar, Russia, Singapore, Trinidad and Tobago, United Arab Emirates and the United States.

Member SWFs elect a chair and two deputy chairs. They are assisted by a professional secretariat. The IFSWF meets at least once a year and is open to the participation of other relevant players as observers. It communicates the outcomes of its activities on its website and with press releases.

Three sub-groups have been created in order to better deal with specific issues:

1.   application of Santiago Principles

2.   investment and risk-management practices

3.   the international investment environment and recipient country relationships.

In October 2009 the IFSWF held its inaugural meeting in Baku, Azerbaijan, hosted by the State Oil Fund of Azerbaijan (SOFAZ). 20 members attended the meeting, along with representatives from several recipient countries, international organisations including the IMF, the European Commission and the OECD and some private-sector companies. On this occasion the forum issued the so-called Baku Statement[199]. This reaffirmed the importance of maintaining an open investment environment at global level, praised countries for pursuing fiscal and monetary support measures for the world economy, encouraged the implementation of reforms in recipient countries' financial sectors to avoid protectionism and to be transparent and nondiscriminatory, and confirmed progress on the application of the Santiago Principles.

It did so, however, without providing any further details of how this was being accomplished or measured. And in spite of all this goodwill, in 2010 the forum had still not provided consistent studies based on concrete information and statistical data from SWFs.

To assess SWFs' degree of compliance with the Santiago Principles we must therefore refer to specific studies that have dealt with this topic. These are covered in the following section.

Do SWFs comply with the Santiago Principles?

Behrendt[200], for example, has defined a Santiago Compliance Index to help assess this. Using publicly available material, this assesses the compliance of the 26 SWFs that belong to the IWG and have subscribed to the principles. Preliminary results (the study was not yet completed at the time of writing) show an uneven level of compliance. Some of the funds are close to full compliance, while most are still quite far away from it (and not in compliance with even 50% of the principles).

As might be expected, the most compliant funds are those that were effectively already compliant before signing up to the principles (the New Zealand Superannuation Fund, Norwegian GPF-G, Australian Future Fund and the Ireland Pension Fund). Funds that improved their position include the CIC, which made significant progress – especially in terms of transparency of financial information – and in 2009 issued its first annual report. The less compliant funds include most from the MENA region: LIA, Bahrain, ADIA, QIA and KIA, plus the Mexico Stabilization Fund and the Botswana Pula Fund. Equatorial Guinea and the Iran Oil Fund are completely opaque.

Figure 18 – Degree of compliance with Santiago Principles (% on all the principles)

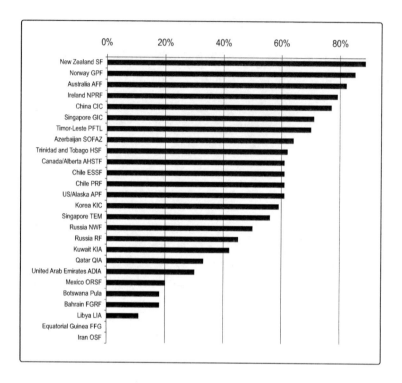

Source: Behrendt (2010).

Behrendt suggests that analysis be made of the correlation between a SWF's level of compliance and owner-countries' form of government. His preliminary study finds a positive correlation between the Santiago Compliance Index and *The Economist* Intelligent Unit's index of democracy 2008[201]. We notice that there are important outliers such as China, Azerbaijan, Botswana and others, which would require further analysis.

Figure 19 – Correlation between Santiago Compliance Index and *The Economist* Intelligent Unit's index of democracy (2008)

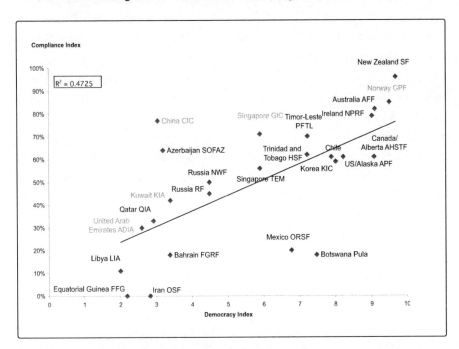

Source: Behrendt (2010). SWFs larger than US$250 billion are marked in light grey.

The author identifies three clusters of SWFs. The first one, on the upper right, includes highly compliant funds, with a compliance index of more than 80%, belonging to democratic governments. The largest among them is the Norwegian GPF-F. The others are the Australian Future Fund, the New Zealand Superannuation Fund and the Ireland Pension Fund. The second group, in the middle of the chart, is the largest. It includes relatively compliant SWFs, many of which come from countries with lower democracy ratings. These include the two Singaporean Funds, CIC, the two Russian Funds, the two Chilean Funds, but also the Alberta Fund, the American Alaska Permanent Fund and KIC. Finally, the last group of under-compliant funds, on the bottom left, includes those funds with the lowest levels of compliance, owned by authoritarian regimes located especially in the Middle East and North Africa. These include ADIA, QIA, Bahrain and LIA.

This figure may recall similar regressions between the Truman index and the index of democracy shown in Chapter 5. Indeed, the Santiago Principles were defined on the basis of the Truman scoreboard.

In terms of policy, Behrendt suggests that radical improvements in the level of compliance by individual SWFs, namely those currently under-compliant, could be the catalyst of broader democratic reforms of the political institutions in their countries of origin. This is especially true for the Middle Eastern SWFs.

The second study we'll look at was carried out by the Investor Responsibility Research Center Institute (IRRC) in conjunction with the RiskMetrics Group[202]. Its data was directly collected from SWFs. This was accomplished through a survey on several issues, ranging from engagement and proxy voting to investment strategies and practices, quality of governance, sensitivity to environmental and social issues and the level of human-resources capabilities. The survey also focused on the level of compliance with the Santiago Principles of the ten largest SWFs, namely ADIA, AGFF, CIC, GIC, GPF-G, KIA, LIA, QIA, NWF and RF, and Temasek.

This study was carried out one year after the IWG members' adoption of the Santiago Principles in October 2008. According to the study, with some exceptions, the level of compliance especially in terms of transparency was not satisfactory. Aside from those funds which already had a high level of compliance before adopting the principles, the others seemed not to have undertaken any effort to improve their compliance since then. A few had started to adapt, but given the short time interval since adoption, they had not yet had time to fully adjust. For this reason other studies would be required in the future to assess the long-term compliance of SWFs.

For some of the principles, either information provided by the funds was insufficient or not disclosed at all, or the principle was too broad to be measured. Therefore an assessment of compliance with these principles was not included in this study. Specifically these include GAPP numbers 1, 3, 5, 6 and 13.

For GAPP 2, 7, 10, 12, 15, 19, regarding disclosure of legal and governance frameworks, auditing procedures, compliance with host country rules and investment objectives, the study records full compliance of all the funds. For GAPP 20 (not taking advantage of government privileges) and 24 (having procedures for monitoring GAPP compliance) the study cites a complete lack of compliance by all the funds. Finally for GAPP 4 (rules for funding and withdrawals), 8, 9 (both on the governance framework), 11 (annual reporting), 14 (relationships with third parties based on economic rationales), 16 (disclosure of governance framework), 17 (disclosure of relevant financial information), 18 (investment policy definition and disclosure), 21 (exercise and disclosure of ownership rights), 22 (risk management) and 23 (performance measurement), compliance was partial. The following table reports the number of compliant funds for each of the 19 GAPP assessed.

Table 4 – Number of compliant SWFs per principle

	No compliance	Partial compliance	Full compliance
GAPP 2 – Policy purpose	0	0	10
GAPP 4 – Funding and withdrawal	2	6	2
GAPP 7 – Ownership role	0	0	10
GAPP 8 – Governing body	2	4	4
GAPP 9 – Management independence	3	1	6
GAPP 10 – Accountability framework	0	0	10
GAPP 11 – Annual report	2	0	8
GAPP 12 – Auditing	0	0	10
GAPP 14 – Third parties	4	3	3
GAPP 15 – Compliance with host countries rules	0	0	10
GAPP 16 – Disclosure of governance framework	1	4	5
GAPP 17 – Disclosure of financial information	4	0	6
GAPP 18 – Investment policy	1	4	5
GAPP 19 – Investment objectives	0	0	10
GAPP 20 – No advantage from government privileges	10	0	0
GAPP 21 – Ownership rights	4	3	3
GAPP 22 – Risk management	4	0	6
GAPP 23 – Performance measurement	4	0	6
GAPP 24 – GAPP monitoring	10	0	0

Source: Mehrpouya, Huang and Barnett (2009).

The following table summarises each fund's level of compliance, distinguishing between full, partial and non-compliance.

Table 5 – Percentage of compliance for each SWF (SWFs are ordered by level of full compliance)

	Full compliance	Partial compliance	No compliance
AGFF	90%	0%	10%
GPF-G	90%	0%	10%
Temasek	79%	10%	10%
GIC	74%	10%	16%
CIC	63%	16%	21%
KIA	53%	32%	16%
LIA	47%	21%	32%
RF & NWF	42%	16%	42%
ADIA	32%	16%	53%
QIA	32%	10%	58%

Source: *Mehrpouya, Huang and Barnett (2009).*

AGFF and GPF-G led the ranking with 90% full compliance and 10% no compliance, followed by Temasek (79% full compliance) and GIC (74% full compliance). The worst performances belong to QIA with 32% full compliance and 58% no compliance and ADIA with 32% full compliance and 53% no compliance.

While this analysis was conducted on the basis of valuable direct contributions from SWFs themselves, it still suggests a high level of subjectivity in interpreting the GAPP principles and the choice of criteria for their assessment.

Both studies cited in this section converge in outlining two overall distinct patterns: on the one hand there are the funds which participated in the IWG that are almost fully compliant with the principles (they complied before adopting them); on the other hand there are the SWFs that were not compliant at the moment of adoption and have not demonstrated a noticeable improvement in their level of compliance. Funds that have demonstrated significant efforts to raise their level of compliance over the year since adoption represent a minority. The largest of these is the Chinese CIC.

The OECD and Guidelines for Recipient Countries

At the same time as the establishment of the IWG, the OECD carried out a parallel process to define guidelines for recipient countries. Its goal was to help keep markets open, and to create a stable and reliable framework for foreign investments in return for a commitment to transparency by SWFs.

Meanwhile, various countries, as we saw in Chapter 6, established their own regulations on inflows of foreign capital. All governments now apply restrictions for sensitive and strategic sectors. These conditions and restrictions legitimately slow inflows of investment; there are no cogent international rules prohibiting barriers to investment, in contrast to the WTO's role in the area of trade. Instead, the number of bilateral investment agreements is increasing, with the risk of fragmenting capital markets.

It is a common belief that developed countries are to blame for this kind of protectionism. The reality is actually rather different. According to the FDI Regulatory Restrictiveness Index[203], calculated by the OECD to measure the level of 'formal' (or statutory) restrictions on foreign investment both for member states and some other non-OECD countries, the countries most open to foreign direct investment are in Europe (Latvia, Belgium, Germany, the UK and Italy ranking in the first five positions as from Figure 20) followed by the other large economies such as Japan and the US. Russia, India and China are at the bottom of the ranking. Paradoxically those countries with some of the largest SWFs are also those with the most restrictive regulations on inflows of foreign investment. In terms of openness to FDI, therefore, there is a notable asymmetry between industrialised countries (especially Europe and North America) and emerging markets, which are much more restrictive. Current assessments, especially journalistic ones, do not adequately point out this situation.

Figure 20 – FDI regulatory restrictiveness (2006)

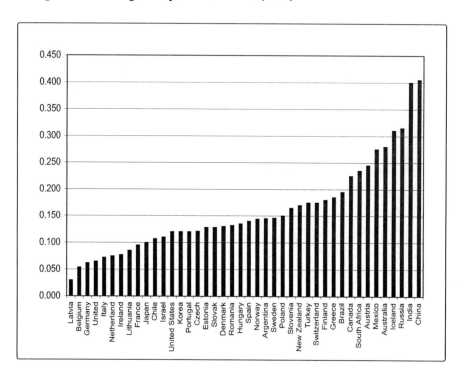

Source: Our elaborations on Koyama and Golub (2006) (OECD).

The OECD's credentials for defining guidelines for recipient countries of FDI are well known. The OECD was the first international forum where good practices for international investment policies were discussed. Sometimes this was a simple code of conduct or a set of guidelines, in other cases it was legally cogent rules supported by member governments. Two of the most significant are the Code of Liberalisation of Capital Movements, adopted in 1961, and the Declaration on International Investment and Multinational Enterprises from 1976, revised in 2000. In addition the OECD also led the attempt to create a multilateral context for redrafting a system of international investment rules with the Multilateral Agreement on Investment (modelled on the WTO's for global trade) negotiated from 1995 to 1998, which then failed due to various pressures.

In April 2008 the OECD's Committee on Foreign Investment, in response to the G7's call for maintaining the openness of international capital markets, presented the report *Sovereign Wealth Funds and Recipient Country Policies*[204] to the ministers of the member countries (from here on simply called the Report). This was part of a larger project called Freedom of Investment, National Security and Strategic Industries (from here on called the Project) launched in 2006 to counter protectionist tendencies and ensure the openness of capital markets to foreign investment.

The Report addressed the OECD's 30 member countries, 15 non-member countries (including China and Russia) and the European Commission on the need to keep capital markets open. Its authors also consulted with representatives of some SWFs. The document was approved by the ministers of the OECD in June 2008[205].

After acknowledging the benefits of SWF investment for recipient countries, home countries and the international financial markets, the OECD Report invited recipient countries to hold to existing, codified principles as laid down in the Code of Liberalisation of Capital Movements, and the Declaration on International Investment and Multinational Enterprises, already adopted by 41 countries (OECD and non-OECD). Specifically[206]:

- non-discrimination of foreign investors versus domestic investors, and of investors from OECD countries versus those from non-OECD countries

- transparency of procedures/regulations limiting foreign investment

- progressive liberalisation of restrictions on capital movement

- commitment not to introduce new restrictions

- unilateral liberalisation not conditioned on the principle of reciprocity.

In the Report the OECD recognised the legitimacy of concerns about national security and the member countries' right to undertake action to protect it. It acknowledged that SWFs had caused particular concern in this area, as they were entities that may act not for purely economic reasons but out of geo-strategic or foreign policy motivations.

Nevertheless the organisation invited its member countries to apply these exceptions for protecting national security carefully, and not to let them become an excuse for lessening their commitment to open capital markets. To this end, in 2006 specific guidelines began to be drafted as part of the Project – not directly pertaining to SWFs, but also applicable to them. They were intended for adoption by governments in drafting and implementing measures aimed at protecting national security from malign or questionable FDI. They express the following principles:[207]

- non-discrimination or equal treatment for investors in similar situations regardless of nationality

- transparency and predictability of rules, procedures, their length, changes to rules, and respect for the confidentiality of information

- regulatory proportionality, which means that restrictions on investment and conditionality of transactions should not be greater than needed to protect national security and should be avoided if existing measures are adequate and appropriate for resolving threats to security

- accountability, which includes procedures for parliamentary oversight, mechanisms for international control, internal judicial review, periodic regulatory impact assessments, and authorisation to block investment only at high government levels (heads of state or ministers).

The guidelines were also accompanied by a peer-review mechanism to which countries subject their own measures currently in force or being drafted and receive feedback on the basis of the established principles.

In October 2008 the final phase of this OECD process led to the adoption by OECD members of a Declaration representing the sum of the documents mentioned so far[208]. This outcome was presented to the International Monetary and Financial Committee meeting in Washington on 11 October 2008. According to the Secretary-General Angel Gurría, the next step would be to monitor the guidelines' observance by recipient countries.

The OECD approach is based on the principle of "not reinventing the wheel"[209], but rather exploiting the organisation's tradition as "the place where new and emerging investment issues have been analysed and debated"[210] for decades. Current instruments were considered adequate, if correctly applied, to provide an open investment environment for SWFs.

The effectiveness of these guidelines depends on several political factors. Liberalisation of markets, including capital markets, slowed significantly due to the 2007-2009 financial crisis.

Another limit stems from the fact that these guidelines are applicable only to OECD members and therefore leave out most SWF home countries and emerging market countries (which are those more inclined to protectionism). These are precisely the countries in greater need of guidelines.

However, the main limit probably lies in the discretion granted to member countries in defining some key (but fuzzy) concepts involved in the guidelines. Not the least of these is what does or doesn't constitute national security, and what does or doesn't constitute an imperilment of it. Member states therefore have ample room to escape the guidelines should the political environment turn sour on foreign investment.

The OECD process therefore represents a voluntary framework based largely on recipient countries' goodwill – just as the Santiago Principles are based on SWFs' goodwill. Voluntarism is the common, and perhaps concerning, theme.

A Multilateral Framework Based on Goodwill: Can it Work?

Acknowledging the voluntary basis of this multilateral framework, attention should turn to identifying incentives that can encourage both SWFs and recipient countries to comply. Since SWF countries are becoming increasingly responsible and willing to share global financial responsibilities, we believe this incentive-based approach is the best means of furthering the implementation of the Santiago Principles. Already, at the OECD level, the process of peer review exercises a certain pressure on individual member states to comply with the guidelines.

We are aware, though, that one must avoid wishful thinking. Disputes may arise, and, in this multilateral framework (IMF and OECD), there is as yet no instrument to resolve controversies. Unfortunately, at this stage such an instrument would be difficult to define and implement. Nevertheless, one international organisation that suggests itself as a reasonable candidate for assuming a regulatory role is the World Trade Organisation (WTO). With its services agreement, the General Agreement on Trade in Services (GATS), which already covers most SWF investment, as well as other agreements, the WTO offers a precedent for designing regulatory disciplines for SWFs and recipient countries as well[211].

Another flaw is the fact that the Santiago Principles are based on a specific definition of SWFs (provided in Chapter 2) that leaves out other state investment vehicles. Sovereign investments of a more political nature may risk being channelled through other vehicles such as state-owned enterprises, thus triggering anyway a protectionist reaction in recipient countries (most of the controversial acquisitions cited in Chapter 5 that prompted worried reactions in the recipient countries had been sponsored by SOEs).

However, we believe that this multilateral IMF-OECD framework is the only feasible and coherent solution, at least for now, in striking a balance between national security concerns and the need to have open capital markets.

The advantages of such a framework, at least in future, could be various if a virtuous circle takes hold in response. If SWFs become more transparent due to compliance with the Santiago Principles, they should be more willingly accepted by recipient countries; recipient countries will be less subject to protectionist pressures and may therefore keep their capital markets more open. In this way an international framework could begin to be established which promotes reciprocal trust between SWFs, home countries and recipient countries and plays a part in achieving the common goal of a global financial market that is stable and open to international investment.

However, we can ask SWFs to be responsible and transparent only insofar as the same will be required of all other actors (i.e. other investment entities) in the global financial markets, which as we have learned from the 2007-2009 crisis, could be much more dangerous for market equilibria than SWFs have ever been.

Conclusion

After 20 years of growing globalisation with its pervasive optimism, the financial and economic crisis of 2007-2009 brought about many changes across the world. These include widespread disenchantment with the free market as the most effective mechanism to deliver economic wellbeing, a new season of government intervention to avoid the collapse of financial institutions, and a call for new and more exacting regulations.

Given this landscape, more stringent rules, more transparency and more responsible actors are needed at the global level to avoid the growth of protectionism which in the long run – as economic history shows – would damage worldwide economic growth. The future of SWFs must be seen from this perspective. If the world economy emerges from the crisis to reinforce international cooperation by reforming institutions and rules together along the lines outlined by the G20, then it is likely that SWFs will adopt the Santiago Principles and recipient countries will apply the OECD's guidelines. This would itself reinforce such international cooperation and reform. All this would be to the advantage of global development, enhancing cooperation between different economies and economic blocs. If, on the other hand, the global economy comes out of the crisis held down by stronger economic nationalism – with entrenched government intervention in economies, as well as trade and investment barriers erected by nation against nation, or bloc against bloc – then SWFs will not have an easy time investing abroad. The only choice will likely be for them to sign specific agreements with individual countries in the form of state – as opposed to market – cooperation.

Whatever the uncertain dynamics of the crisis and its outcome, some conclusions can, however, be reached about the present and future of SWFs. As we have seen throughout this book, though confusion about them is (not without reason) somewhat common, several key features and trends of SWFs can be established. They are worth drawing together again as we close.

1. SWFs can be established with different goals. They are a non-homogeneous category of financial player, characterised by highly differentiated legal and institutional status, declared and pursued objectives, and strategies and operating modes on international financial markets.

2. Most of them originate from rent or quasi-rent positions, and therefore their main need is to invest in activities capable of producing long-term, risk-balanced returns.

3. The origin of SWFs mainly in emerging economies and the hoarding of financial exchange reserves in the hands of these governments symbolises a broader shift of economic power from West to East.

4. To date, empirical evidence indicates that SWFs have behaved as economically rational investors who seek to maximise their profits through the proper combination of risk and return. They are recognised as contributing to the stability of the financial system – in fact they exhibited anti-cyclical behaviour during the 2007-2009 financial downturn. This is due to their long-term horizons, the greater diversification of their portfolios, their average low level of indebtedness, and the absence of liquidity risks. Moreover there is no empirical evidence so far proving they have acted on the basis of anything other than economic motivations. On the other hand, considering the size of SWFs and the consequent potential for imitative or 'herd' behaviour, their opacity, and the fact that they are not regulated, they can also be potentially destabilising for the markets. At least for now, evidence seems to suggest that their stabilising factors outweigh the destabilising ones; but this evidence is not univocal and further research is required.

5. SWFs are not unbeatable giants – but they are strong. They did not escape the financial storm of 2007-2009 and suffered large losses on their investments in the US and European banking and financial sector. However, after a period of retrenchment they returned with appropriately adjusted targets and strategies. Most of their losses were not realised.

They are therefore alive and well, and their considerable influence on financial markets seems destined to last some time.

6. The transparency of SWFs is still far below Western standards. The IMF's Santiago Principles are important but their potential should not be overestimated. The financial crisis of 2007-2009 of course also demonstrated that, in Western countries as well as in the developing nations, financial transparency and governance still leaves a lot to be desired wherever in the world you are. The need to improve governance mechanisms and transparency must therefore be addressed with a symmetrical approach: including all the global players that interact on the financial markets and avoiding any double standards. Moreover, while the issue of transparency is usually debated from the viewpoint of Western countries, it is clear that the interests of citizens in SWF home countries must also be taken into account.

7. SWFs' renewed investment strategies must necessarily take into account the long-term development needs of their own countries and regions, the diversification of their economies, and advances in technology and knowledge. Indeed SWFs are increasingly subject to the scrutiny of their own domestic public opinion. The Persian Gulf countries should consider that, with their enormous wealth in sovereign funds, combined with European manufacturing capacity and technology, they could provide a formidable contribution to the development of Mediterranean Africa and the Middle East. Russia, the Eurasian giant, could and should also do more to develop domestically. And China and Singapore could contribute more to the growth of less-developed Asian countries.

8. Different approaches can be identified at the national level in the EU. But the approach provided by the European Commission generally prevails at the time of writing, which warns member states not to breach EU law and recommends they avoid undertaking new legislative initiatives individually

– arguing that doing so would damage EU cohesion and waste the opportunity to receive fresh liquidity into the European economy. In this respect we propose that the EMU should also establish its own sovereign wealth fund to promote growth domestically and abroad.

9. Striking the balance between the benefits SWFs may provide for the economic-financial system, and their supposed potential for jeopardising national security, is something that can only be partially carried out at a national level. In so doing, the risk is inevitably run that individual, uncoordinated and politically-driven reactions enact a drift towards protectionism and the fragmentation of the global financial market. The IMF-OECD multilateral framework based on goodwill represents, at this stage, the only feasible and coherent solution for striking a balance between national security concerns and the need to have open capital markets. However, we can ask SWFs to be responsible and transparent only as far as the same will be required for all the other actors on global financial markets. This, as the 2007-2009 crisis proved, may be even more challenging.

10. SWFs are good news for the global economy, as major and minor players seek to find the way ahead in the wake of the 2007-2009 crisis. With laissez-faire economics seemingly discredited, along with the false spread of economic growth based solely on short-sighted financial innovation with no consistent evaluation of risk, the search (ad hoc and deliberate) for surer foundations has begun. For this to be successful, it cannot be reduced to US-Chinese bilateralism (although both countries must certainly reduce their symmetrical imbalances). It must be achieved multilaterally. And other countries, and in particular the EU, can and must pursue a cooperative course as opposed to the confrontational one that too often unfolds. In all this, SWFs sit as investors with a remarkable and pervasive influence on financial markets, with trillions of dollars at their disposal, and the prosperity of future generations seemingly their overriding concern. Since the adoption of the Santiago Principles and the establishment of

their own forum (IFSWF), they appear increasingly willing to assume the role of responsible actors more involved in shaping the financial and monetary global framework. Such varied, long-term, significant and (with good fortune and pressure) increasingly conscientious investors – for all the suspicions they have provoked – will almost certainly only be a force for good.

Appendix
The Santiago Principles

Generally Accepted Principles and Practices (GAPP) – the 'Santiago Principles'

GAPP 1. Principle

The legal framework for the SWF should be sound and support its effective operation and the achievement of its stated objective(s).

GAPP 1.1. Subprinciple. The legal framework for the SWF should ensure legal soundness of the SWF and its transactions.

GAPP 1.2. Subprinciple. The key features of the SWF's legal basis and structure, as well as the legal relationship between the SWF and other state bodies, should be publicly disclosed.

GAPP 2. Principle

The policy purpose of the SWF should be clearly defined and publicly disclosed.

GAPP 3. Principle

Where the SWF's activities have significant direct domestic macroeconomic implications, those activities should be closely coordinated with the domestic fiscal and monetary authorities, so as to ensure consistency with the overall macroeconomic policies.

GAPP 4. Principle

There should be clear and publicly disclosed policies, rules, procedures, or arrangements in relation to the SWF's general approach to funding, withdrawal, and spending operations.

GAPP 4.1. Subprinciple. The source of SWF funding should be publicly disclosed.

GAPP 4.2. Subprinciple. The general approach to withdrawals from the SWF and spending on behalf of the government should be publicly disclosed.

GAPP 5. Principle

The relevant statistical data pertaining to the SWF should be reported on a timely basis to the owner, or as otherwise required, for inclusion where appropriate in macroeconomic data sets.

GAPP 6. Principle

The governance framework for the SWF should be sound and establish a clear and effective division of roles and responsibilities in order to facilitate accountability and operational independence in the management of the SWF to pursue its objectives.

GAPP 7. Principle

The owner should set the objectives of the SWF, appoint the members of its governing body(ies) in accordance with clearly defined procedures, and exercise oversight over the SWF's operations.

GAPP 8. Principle

The governing body(ies) should act in the best interests of the SWF, and have a clear mandate and adequate authority and competency to carry out its functions.

GAPP 9. Principle

The operational management of the SWF should implement the SWF's strategies in an independent manner and in accordance with clearly defined responsibilities.

GAPP 10. Principle

The accountability framework for the SWF's operations should be clearly defined in the relevant legislation, charter, other constitutive documents, or management agreement.

GAPP 11. Principle

An annual report and accompanying financial statements on the SWF's operations and performance should be prepared in a timely fashion and in accordance with recognised international or national accounting standards in a consistent manner.

GAPP 12. Principle

The SWF's operations and financial statements should be audited annually in accordance with recognised international or national auditing standards in a consistent manner.

GAPP 13. Principle

Professional and ethical standards should be clearly defined and made known to the members of the SWF's governing body(ies), management, and staff.

GAPP 14. Principle

Dealing with third parties for the purpose of the SWF's operational management should be based on economic and financial grounds, and follow clear rules and procedures.

GAPP 15. Principle

SWF operations and activities in host countries should be conducted in compliance with all applicable regulatory and disclosure requirements of the countries in which they operate.

GAPP 16. Principle

The governance framework and objectives, as well as the manner in which the SWF's management is operationally independent from the owner, should be publicly disclosed.

GAPP 17. Principle

Relevant financial information regarding the SWF should be publicly disclosed to demonstrate its economic and financial orientation, so as to contribute to stability in international financial markets and enhance trust in recipient countries.

GAPP 18. Principle

The SWF's investment policy should be clear and consistent with its defined objectives, risk tolerance, and investment strategy, as set by the owner or the governing body(ies), and be based on sound portfolio management principles.

GAPP 18.1. Subprinciple. The investment policy should guide the SWF's financial risk exposures and the possible use of leverage.

GAPP 18.2. Subprinciple. The investment policy should address the extent to which internal and/or external investment managers are used, the range of their activities and authority, and the process by which they are selected and their performance monitored.

GAPP 18.3. Subprinciple. A description of the investment policy of the SWF should be publicly disclosed.

GAPP 19. Principle

The SWF's investment decisions should aim to maximise risk-adjusted financial returns in a manner consistent with its investment policy, and based on economic and financial grounds.

GAPP 19.1. Subprinciple. If investment decisions are subject to other than economic and financial considerations, these should be clearly set out in the investment policy and be publicly disclosed.

GAPP 19.2. Subprinciple. The management of an SWF's assets should be consistent with what is generally accepted as sound asset management principles.

GAPP 20. Principle

The SWF should not seek or take advantage of privileged information or inappropriate influence by the broader government in competing with private entities.

GAPP 21. Principle

SWFs view shareholder ownership rights as a fundamental element of their equity investments' value. If an SWF chooses to exercise its ownership rights, it should do so in a manner that is consistent with its investment policy and protects the financial value of its investments. The SWF should publicly disclose its general approach to voting securities of listed entities, including the key factors guiding its exercise of ownership rights.

GAPP 22. Principle

The SWF should have a framework that identifies, assesses, and manages the risks of its operations.

GAPP 22.1. Subprinciple. The risk management framework should include reliable information and timely reporting systems, which should enable the adequate monitoring and management of relevant risks within acceptable parameters and levels, control and incentive mechanisms, codes of conduct, business continuity planning, and an independent audit function.

GAPP 22.2. Subprinciple. The general approach to the SWF's risk management framework should be publicly disclosed.

GAPP 23. Principle

The assets and investment performance (absolute and relative to benchmarks, if any) of the SWF should be measured and reported to the owner according to clearly defined principles or standards.

GAPP 24. Principle

A process of regular review of the implementation of the GAPP should be engaged in by or on behalf of the SWF.

Notes

[1] Nugée (2009), p. 4.

[2] Griffith-Jones and Ocampo (2008).

[3] Ibid.

[4] Aizenman J. (2007).

[5] Obstfeld, Shambaugh and Taylor (2008).

[6] Rodrik D. (2006).

[7] Rozanov (2005).

[8] Nugée (2009), p.4.

[9] Rozanov (2005).

[10] Kern (2008).

[11] Ibid.

[12] Miracky and Bortolotti (2009).

[13] Quadrio Curzio and Miceli (2009).

[14] Kern (2009).

[15] Bortolotti, Fotak, Megginson and Miracky (2009).

[16] IWG [IMF] (2008b).

[17] Ibid, p.3.

[18] Blundell-Wignall, Hu and Yermo (2008).

[19] Truman (2008a).

[20] IMF (2008b).

[21] There are several other estimates of losses suffered by SWFs in this period. For example, according to Kern, a 'typical' SWF equity portfolio may have lost 45% between end-2007 and early 2009. The loss resulting from our estimates is significantly lower, not only due to the effect of the presence in the portfolio of rather diversified financial instruments in addition to equity, but also because most SWFs, with some exceptions, have not realised their losses, and are holding on to their investments. In addition, for some funds such as the Norwegian GPF-G, data from September 2009 already incorporates equity markets' rebound of mid-2009.

[22] Quadrio Curzio and Miceli (2009).

[23] Ibid.

[24] British Petroleum (2009).

[25] IMF, *World Economic Outlook Database*, updated October, accessed January 2010.

[26] SAFE, institutional website:

www.safe.gov.cn/model_safe_en/tjsj_en/tjsj_detail_en.jsp?ID=30303000000000000,18&id=4

[27] IMF, *World Economic Outlook Database*, updated October, accessed January 2010.

[28] IMF (2008a).

[29] Ibid.

[30] Ibid.

[31] Ibid.

[32] IMF, Cofer Database, accessed January 2010.

[33] IMF (2008a).

[34] Ibid.

[35] Kern (2009).

[36] Ibid.

[37] Ibid.

[38] Jen (2007).

[39] Kern (2008).

[40] Fernandez and Eschweiler (2008).

[41] Lyons (2007).

[42] IMF, World Economic Outlook database, updated October 2009, accessed January 2010.

[43] Setser and Ziemba (2009).

[44] IMF, World Economic Outlook database, updated October 2009, accessed January 2010.

[45] SAFE, institutional website:

www.safe.gov.cn/model_safe_en/tjsj_en/tjsj_detail_en.jsp?ID=30303000000000000,18&id=4

[46] Cang and Miles (2009).

[47] It is interesting to note that Quadrio Curzio's book (1982) was translated into Chinese in 1988.

[48] Jen and Andreopoulos (2008).

[49] Subacchi (2009).

[50] Kern (2009).

[51] Quadrio Curzio and Miceli (2009).

[52] This estimate is in line with Ziemba (2009). According to Ziemba: "The foreign assets of GCC central banks and sovereign funds are estimated to have fallen to just over $1.1 trillion at the end of June 2009 from about $1.2 trillion at the end of 2008".

[53] Quadrio Curzio and Miceli (2009).

[54] IWG [IMF] (2008b); Balding (2008); Ziemba (2008); Setser and Ziemba (2009); Barbary and Chin (2009); Sovereign Wealth Fund Institute, institutional website.

[55] Truman (2008a).

[56] Setser and Ziemba (2009).

[57] Kawach (2009).

[58] Backfisch (2010).

[59] Ziemba (2008).

[60] Backfisch (2010).

[61] Ibid.

[62] Barbary and Chin (2009).

[63] Mubadala, official website: www.mubadala.ae

[64] Barbary V. and Chin E. (2009).

[65] Mubadala (2008).

[66] IPIC, official website: www.ipic.ae/en/home

[67] Miracky, Barbary, Fotak, and Bortolotti (2009).

[68] Ibid.

[69] Barbary and Chin (2009).

[70] Setser and Ziemba (2009).

[71] In both cases we refer to Goldstein and Pananond (2008), as well as material provided by Temasek and GIC from their websites, reworking it according to our criteria.

[72] Demange (2009).

[73] Ibid.

[74] Clark and Monk (2009a).

[75] GIC (2009).

[76] Ibid.

[77] China Investment Corporation (2009).

[78] Altbach and Cognato (2008); Martin (2008); Marin (2009).

[79] SAFE, institutional website:

www.safe.gov.cn/model_safe_en/tjsj_en/tjsj_detail_en.jsp?ID=30303000000000000,18&id=4

[80] Xiaohong O. and Peng L. (2009).

[81] Miracky, Barbary, Fotak, and Bortolotti (2009).

[82] Anderlini (2009).

[83] GPF-G (2009).

[84] Clark and Monk (2009b).

[85] Backer (2009).

[86] Chesterman (2008).

[87] Clark and Monk (2009b).

[88] Backer (2009).

[89] Clark and Monk (2009b).

[90] Chevrier (2009).

[91] Ibid.

[92] Ministry of Finance of the Russian Federation, institutional website, as at 01/12/2009, available at: www1.minfin.ru/en/nationalwealthfund/

[93] Ibid.

[94] Tovkailo and Pismennaya (2010).

[95] Ministry of Finance of the Russian Federation, institutional website, as at 01/12/2009, available at: www1.minfin.ru/en/nationalwealthfund/

[96] See www.themoscowtimes.com/business/article/376518.html

[97] Ministry of Finance of the Russian Federation, institutional website, as at 01/12/2009, available at: www1.minfin.ru/en/nationalwealthfund/

[98] Miracky and Bortolotti (2009).

[99] Miracky, Barbary, Fotak and Bortolotti (2009).

[100] Kern (2008) and (2009).

[101] Kern's study is based on Dealogic data.

[102] Kern (2009).

[103] Miracky and Bortolotti (2009).

[104] Miracky, Barbary, Fotak and Bortolotti (2009).

[105] Miracky and Bortolotti (2009).

[106] Ibid.

[107] Balding (2008).

[108] Chhaochharia and Laeven (2009).

[109] Kern (2009).

[110] Miracky and Bortolotti (2009).

[111] For more details on the shareholdings of single SWFs, see Chapter 3.

[112] Kern (2009).

[113] IWG [IMF] (2008a).

[114] Kotter and Lel (2008).

[115] IWG [IMF] (2008a)

[116] Jen (2008).

[117] Kern (2009).

[118] Miracky and Bortolotti (2009).

[119] Beck and Fidora (2008).

[120] Kotter and Lel (2008).

[121] Dewenter, Han and Malatesta (2009).

[122] Bortolotti, Fotak, Megginson and Miracky (2009).

[123] Chhaochharia and Laeven (2009).

[124] Knill, Lee and Mauck (2009b).

[125] Sun and Hesse (2009).

[126] Fernandes (2009).

[127] Bernstein, Lerner and Schoar (2009).

[128] Jen and Miles (2007).

[129] Gieve (2008).

[130] Galani and Nixon (2008).

[131] Summers (2007).

[132] Setser (2008a).

[133] *The Economist* Intelligence Unit (2008).

[134] Röller and Veron (2008).

[135] Drezner (2008).

[136] Ibid.

[137] IMF (2009).

[138] For more details, see Chapter 4.

[139] Kern (2009).

[140] Miracky, Dyer, Fisher, Goldner, Lagarde and Piedrahita (2008).

[141] Kern (2009).

[142] Miracky and Bortolotti (2009).

[143] IWG [IMF] (2008a).

[144] Truman (2008a).

[145] Balding (2008).

[146] Chhaochharia and Laeven (2009).

[147] Anderlini (2008).

[148] Beck and Fidora (2008).

[149] Knill, Lee and Mauck (2009a).

[150] Karolyi and Liao (2009).

[151] Avendaño and Santiso (2009).

[152] Truman (2007) and (2008b).

[153] Monk (2008).

[154] Ibid.

[155] Clark (2009).

[156] Truman (2008a).

[157] Balding (2009).

[158] Beck and Fidora (2008).

[159] Setser (2008b).

[160] Bertoni (2008).

[161] Aizenman and Glick (2008).

[162] Kaufmann, Kraay and Mastruzzi (2007).

[163] Lyons (2007).

[164] Behrendt (2009).

[165] Khouri (2009).

[166] Blackburn, Del Vecchio, Fox, Gatenio, Khayum, and Wolfson (2008).

[167] Marchick and Slaughter (2008).

[168] UNCTAD, Foreign Direct Investment Database On-line, accessed February 2010.

[169] Information on CFIUS can be found at United States Department of Treasury institutional website: www.treas.gov/offices/international-affairs/cfius/

[170] US Department of Treasury, (2007), Semiannual Report on International Economic and Exchange Rate Policies, June 2007, Appendix III.

[171] An appendix on SWFs was also attached to all the subsequent reports of the same series until December 2008.

[172] UNCTAD, Foreign Direct Investment Database On-line, accessed February 2010.

[173] CFIUS (2008) and (2009).

[174] Gilson and Milhaupt (2008).

[175] Keller (2009).

[176] Epstein and Rose (2009).

[177] Eurostat, Economy and Finance Database, accessed February 2010.

[178] Freshfields Bruckhaus Deringer (2009).

[179] Demarolle (2008) and (2009).

[180] Eubusiness (2008).

[181] Barbary and Chin (2009).

[182] Kern (2009).

[183] European Commission (2008).

[184] Council of the European Union (2008).

[185] European Parliament (2008).

[186] For example: Gugler and Chaisse (2009); Prost, Parmentier and Hugon (2009).

[187] Barysch, Tilford and Whyte (2008).

[188] Röller and Veron (2008).

[189] Demarolle (2008).

[190] Bassanini and Reviglio (2009).

[191] Quadrio Curzio (2008); Quadrio Curzio and Miceli (2008).

[192] IMF, Data Template on International Reserves and Foreign Currency Liquidity, accessed February 2010.

[193] Quadrio Curzio (2009).

[194] Cohen (2009).

[195] G8 Summit of June 2007 at Heiligendamm (G8, (2007)); G7 of Finance Ministers October 2007 (G7 Finance Ministers, (2007)); US Department of Treasury (2008); IMF (2008b).

[196] IWG [IMF] (2008b).

[197] Truman (2008a).

[198] IWG (2009).

[199] ISFWF (2009).

[200] Behrendt (2010).

[201] *The Economist* Intelligence Unit (2008).

[202] Mehrpouya, Huang and Barnett (2009).

[203] Koyama and Golub (2006).

[204] OECD (2008e).

[205] OECD (2008a).

[206] OECD (2008b).

[207] OECD (2008d).

[208] OECD (2008c).

[209] Gurría (2008).

[210] Ibid.

[211] Mattoo and Subramanian (2008).

Bibliography

Aizenman J. (2007), 'Large Hoarding of International Reserves and the Emerging Global Economic Architecture', NBER Working Paper, n. 13277, July.

Aizenman J. and Glick R. (2008), 'Sovereign Wealth Funds: Stylized Facts about Their Determinants and Governance', NBER Working Paper, December.

Alaska Permanent Fund (2009), Monthly Financial Statement, November, available at www.apfc.org/ amiReportsArchive/APFC200911.pdf

Altbach E.G. and Cognato M. (2008), 'Understanding China's New Sovereign Wealth Fund', NBR Analysis, The National Bureau of Asian Research, vol. 19, n. 1, July.

Anderlini J. (2008), 'Beijing Uses Forex Reserves to Target Taiwan,' in *Financial Times*, September 12.

Anderlini J. (2009), 'China Considers extra $200bn for CIC Sovereign Wealth Fund', in *Financial Times*, December 21.

Avendaño R. and Santiso J. (2009), 'Are sovereign wealth funds' investments politically biased? A comparison with mutual funds', OECD Development Centre, Working Paper No. 283, December.

Backer L. (2009), 'Sovereign Wealth Funds as Regulatory Chameleons: The Norwegian Sovereign Wealth Funds and Public Global Governance Through Private Global Investment', in Social Science Research Network (SSRN).

Backfisch M. (2010), Interview with Sheikh Ahmed Bin Zayed Al Nehayan, in *Handelsblatt*, January 11.

Balding C. (2008), 'A Portfolio Analysis of Sovereign Wealth Funds', Working Paper, University of California, Irvine.

Balding C. (2009), 'Framing Sovereign Wealth Funds: What We Know and Need to Know', in Social Science Research Network (SSRN).

Barbary V. and Chin E. (2009), 'Testing Time. Sovereign Wealth Funds In The Middle East & North Africa And The Global Financial Crisis', Monitor Group Report.

Barysch K., Tilford S. and Whyte P. (2008), 'State, Money and Rules: An EU Policy for Sovereign Investments', Centre for European Reform, December.

Bassanini F. and Reviglio E. (2009), 'Long-Term Investments. The European Answer to the Crisis. Towards a New European Policy of Value Creation for Future Generations:

the "Marguerite" Network', Paris Conference For Long-Term Value & Economic Stability, Paris, June 22.

Beck R. and Fidora M. (2008), 'The Impact of Sovereign Wealth Funds on Global Financial Markets', ECB Occasional Paper, series n. 91, June.

Behrendt S. (2009), 'An Update on Arab Sovereign Wealth Funds', in Behrendt S. and Kodmani B. (eds), 2009, *Managing Arab Sovereign Wealth in Turbulent Times—and Beyond*, Carnegie Papers N° 16, Carnegie Endowment for International Peace, pp.3-8.

Behrendt S. (2010), 'Sovereign Wealth Funds: The Governance Challenge', Carnegie Endowment for International Peace, International Economic Bulletin, January, available at: www.carnegieendowment.org/publications/index.cfm?fa=view&id=24757

Bernstein S., Lerner J. and Schoar A. (2009), 'The Investment Strategies of Sovereign Wealth Funds', Harvard Business School, Working Paper 09-112, in Social Science Research Network (SSRN).

Bertoni F. (2008), 'Sovereign funds and the process of international financial integration; stepping stones or stumbling blocks?', in *Osservatorio monetario*, n. 3, Laboratorio di Analisi Monetaria, Università Cattolica del Sacro Cuore, Milan, pp. 31-41.

Blackburn J., Del Vecchio B., Fox I., Gatenio C., Khayum O. and Wolfson D. (2008), 'Do Sovereign Wealth Funds Best Serve the Interests of their Respective Citizens?', University of Chicago, Graduate School of Business, Social Science Research Network (SSRN).

Blundell-Wignall, A., Y. Hu and J. Yermo (2008), 'Sovereign Wealth and Pension Fund Issues', OECD Working Papers on Insurance and Private Pensions, No. 14, OECD Publishing.

Bortolotti B., Fotak V., Megginson W. and Miracky W. (2009), 'Sovereign Wealth Fund Investment. Patterns and Performance', Fondazione Eni Enrico Mattei, Nota di Lavoro 22.2009, April.

British Petroleum (2009), *British Petroleum Statistical Review of World Energy*.

Cang A. and Miles T. (2009), 'China admits to building up stockpile of gold', *Reuters*, Friday, April 24.

Chesterman S. (2008), 'The Turn to Ethics: Disinvestment from Multinational Corporations for Human Rights Violations – The Case of Norway's Sovereign Wealth Fund', in *Public Law & Legal Theory Research Paper Series*, Working Paper No. 08-25 and in Social Science Research Network (SSRN).

Chevrier C. (2009), 'Sovereign Wealth Funds in Russia', in *Revue d'Economie Financière*, special issue 2009: Sovereign Wealth Funds, pp. 75-83.

Chhaochharia V. and Laeven L. (2008), 'Sovereign Wealth Funds: Their Investment Strategies and Performance', CEPR Discussion Paper N°DP6959.

Chhaochharia V. and Laeven L. (2009), 'The Investment Allocation of Sovereign Wealth Funds', in Social Science Research Network (SSRN).

China Investment Corporation (2009), Annual Report 2008, available at: www.china-inv.cn/cicen/annals/annals.html

CFIUS (2008), Annual Report to Congress, Public version, December.

CFIUS (2009), Annual Report to Congress, Public version, November.

Clark G. (2009), 'Temptation and the virtues of long-term commitment: the governance of sovereign wealth fund investment', in Social Science Research Network (SSRN).

Clark G. and Monk A. (2009a), 'Government of Singapore Investment Corporation (GIC): Insurer of last resort and bulwark of nation-state legitimacy', in Social Science Research Network (SSRN).

Clark G. and Monk A. (2009b), 'Resource wealth and the ethics of global investment: The legitimacy and governance of Norway's sovereign wealth fund', in Social Science Research Network (SSRN).

Cognato M. (2008), 'Understanding China's New Sovereign Wealth Fund', National Bureau of Asian Research, July.

Cohen B. (2009), 'Sovereign Wealth Funds and National Security: The Great Trade-off', paper presented at the annual meeting of the ISA's (the International Studies Association) 50th annual convention 'Exploring The Past, Anticipating The Future', New York Marriott Marquis, NEW YORK CITY, NY, USA, February 15.

Council of the European Union (2008), Presidency Conclusions, Brussels, March 13-14, 7652/1/08 REV1, May 20.

Demange J.M. (2009), 'SWFs in South East Asia', in Revue d'Economie Financière, special issue: Sovereign Wealth Funds, pp. 85-98.

Demarolle A. (2008), 'Rapport sur les Fonds Souverains'.

Demarolle A. (2009), 'Fonds souverains: quelle stratégie pour la France?', in Revue d'Economie Financière, special issue: Sovereign Wealth Funds, pp. 367-372.

Dewenter K. L., Han X. and Malatesta P.H. (2009), 'Firm Value and Sovereign Wealth Fund Investments', University of Washington Working Paper, in Social Science Research Network (SSRN).

Drezner D. (2008), 'Sovereign Wealth Funds And The (In)Security Of Global Finance', in Journal of International Affairs, Fall/Winter, Vol. 62, No. 1, pp. 115-130.

The Economist Intelligence Unit (2008), Index of Democracy 2008, *The Economist*, available at graphics.eiu.com/PDF/Democracy%20Index%202008.pdf

Epstein R. and Rose A. (2009), 'The Regulation of Sovereign Wealth Funds: The Virtues of Going Slow', in *The University of Chicago Law Review*, Vol. 76, No. 1 (Winter), pp. 111-134.

Eubusiness (2008), 'France's Sarkozy calls for European sovereign wealth funds', October 21.

European Commission (2008), 'A Common European Approach to Sovereign Wealth Funds', Communication from the Commission to the European Parliament, the Council, the European Economic and Social Committee and the Committee of the Regions, COM/2008/0115 final, February 27.

European Parliament, Resolution of 9 July 2008 on sovereign wealth funds, P6_TA(2008)0355.

Fernandes N. (2009), 'Sovereign Wealth Funds: Investment Choices and Implications around the World', in Social Science Research Network (SSRN).

Fernandez D.G. and Eschweiler B. (2008), 'Sovereign Wealth Funds: A Bottom-up Primer', JP Morgan Research.

Freshfields Bruckhaus Deringer (2009), 'New restrictions on foreign investments in Germany', Briefing, May.

G7 Finance Ministers (2007), Statement of G-7 Finance Ministers and Central Bank Governors, Washington, October 19.

G8 (2007), 'Growth and responsibility in the world economy', G-8 summit documents, Heiligendamm, Germany, June 6-8.

Galani U. and Nixon S. (2008), 'Don't Fear the Sovereigns', in *The Wall Street Journal*, January 26.

GIC (2009), Report on the Management of the Government's Portfolio for the Year 2008/09, available at: www.gic.com.sg/PDF/GIC_Report_2009.pdf

Gieve J. (2008), 'Sovereign Wealth Funds and Global Imbalances', Bank of England, Quarterly Bulletin, Q2.

Gilson R. and Milhaupt C. (2008), 'Sovereign Wealth Funds and Corporate Governance: A Minimalist Response to the New Mercantilism', in Social Science Research Network (SSRN).

Goldstein A. and Pananond P. (2008), 'Singapore Inc. Goes Shopping Abroad: Profits and Pitfalls', in *Journal of Contemporary Asia*, Vol. 38, No. 3, August, pp. 417–438.

Government of Alberta (2009), 'Alberta Heritage Savings Trust Fund, 2009-2010 Second Quarter', available at:
www.finance.alberta.ca/business/ahstf/2009_2ndq/report.pdf

GPF-G (2009), 'Quarterly Report – Third Quarter 2009', available at:
www.norges-bank.no/templates/reportroot____65330.aspx

Griffith-Jones S. and Ocampo J.A. (2008), 'Sovereign Wealth Funds: A Developing Country Perspective', Paper prepared for the workshop on Sovereign Wealth Funds organised by the Andean Development Corporation, London, February 18, in Social Science Research Network (SSRN).

Gugler P. and Chaisse J. (2009), 'Sovereign Wealth Funds in the European Union. General trust despite concerns', NCCR Trade Working Paper, N° 2009/4, in Social Science Research Network (SSRN).

Gurría A. (2008), 'Keeping markets open for sovereign wealth fund investment', Remarks during a briefing with the United States Council for International Business, available at:
www.oecd.org/document/9/0,3343,en_2649_34887_41492169_1_1_1_1,00.html

Hoguet G.R., Nugée J. and Rozanov A. (2009), Sovereign Wealth Funds, 'Emerging from the financial crisis', in *Vision*, vol. IV, issue 1, State Street Corporation, Boston.

IMF (2008a), *Global Financial Stability Report*.

IMF (2008b), 'Sovereign Wealth Funds. A Work Agenda', prepared by the Monetary and Capital Markets and Policy Development and Review Departments, February 29.

IMF (2009), *Global Financial Stability Report*.

ISFWF (2009), 'Sovereign Wealth Funds Issue "Baku Statement" Reaffirming the Need for Maintaining Open Investment Environment', press release, October 9.

IWG [IMF] (2008a), Current Institutional and Operational Practices.

IWG [IMF] (2008b), Sovereign Wealth Funds – Generally Accepted Principles and Practices – Santiago Principles, October.

IWG (2009), '"Kuwait Declaration": Establishment of the International Forum of Sovereign Wealth Funds', April 9.

Jen S. (2007a), 'How Big Could Sovereign Wealth Funds Be by 2015?', Morgan Stanley Global Research, May 4.

Jen S. (2007b), 'The Definition of a Sovereign Wealth Fund', Morgan Stanley Global Research.

Jen S. (2008), 'How Much Assets Could SWFs Farm Out?', Morgan Stanley Global Research, January 11.

Jen S. and Andreopoulos S. (2008), 'SWFs: Growth Tempered – USD 10 Trillion by 2015', Morgan Stanley Research.

Jen S. and Miles D. (2007), 'Sovereign Wealth Funds and Bond and Equity Prices', Morgan Stanley Research, May 31.

Karolyi G.A. and Liao R.C. (2009), 'What is Different about Government-Controlled Acquirers in Cross-Border Acquisitions?', Working paper, Cornell University and Rutgers University.

Kaufmann D., Kraay A. and Mastruzzi M. (2007), 'Governance Matters VI: Aggregate and Individual Governance Indicators', 1996–2006, World Bank Working Paper WPS4280.

Kawach N. (2009), 'UAE's overseas investment income to rebound in 2009', in *Emirates Business 24/7*, April 20.

Keller A. (2009), 'Sovereign Wealth Funds: Trustworthy Investors or Vehicles of Strategic Ambition? An Assessment of the Benefits, Risks and Possible Regulation of Sovereign Wealth Funds', in Social Science Research Network (SSRN).

Kern S. (2008), 'SWFs and Foreign Investment Policies. An Update,' Deutsche Bank Research, October.

Kern S. (2009), 'Sovereign wealth funds – state investments during the financial crisis', Deutsche Bank Research, July.

Khouri R. G. (2009), 'Whose Sovereignty? Whose Wealth?', in Behrendt S. and Kodmani B. (eds.), 2009, *Managing Arab Sovereign Wealth in Turbulent Times—and Beyond*, Carnegie Papers N° 16, Carnegie Endowment for International Peace, pp.9-12.

Knill A., Lee B. and Mauck N. (2009a), 'Bilateral Political Relations and the Impact of Sovereign Wealth Fund Investment: A Study of Causality', in Social Science Research Network (SSRN).

Knill A., Lee B. and Mauck N. (2009b), '"Sleeping with the Enemy" or "An Ounce of Prevention": Sovereign Wealth Fund Investments and Market Destabilization', Working Paper, Florida State University, in Social Science Research Network (SSRN).

Koyama T. and Golub S. (2006), 'OECD's FDI Regulatory Restrictiveness Index: Revision And Extension To More Economies', Economics Department Working Papers No. 525, ECO/WKP(2006)53.

Kotter J. and Lel U. (2008), 'Friends or Foes? The Stock Price Impact of Sovereign Wealth Fund Investments and the Price of Keeping Secrets', Board of Governors of the Federal Reserves System, International Finance Discussion Papers, n. 940, August.

Laboratorio di Analisi Monetaria – Università Cattolica del Sacro Cuore (2008), Osservatorio monetario, n. 3.

Lyons G. (2007), 'State Capitalism: The rise of sovereign wealth funds, Standard Chartered', November 13.

Marchick D.M. and Slaughter M.J. (2008), Global FDI Policy. 'Correcting a Protectionist Drift', Council on Foreign Relations, CSR N° 34, June.

Marin Y. (2009), 'Chinese Sovereign Wealth Fund: Past, Present and Future', in *Revue d'Economie Financière*, special issue: *Sovereign Wealth Funds*, pp 109-119.

Martin M. (2008), CRE Report for Congress: China's Sovereign Wealth Fund, US Congressional Research Service Report for Congress, January.

Mattoo A. and Subramanian A. (2008), 'Currency Undervaluation and Sovereign Wealth Funds: A New Role for the World Trade Organization', Peterson Institute Working Paper Series WP 08-2.

Mehrpouya A., Huang C. and Barnett T. (2009), 'An Analysis of Proxy Voting and Engagement Policies and Practices of the Sovereign Wealth Funds', IRRC Institute and RiskMetrics Group.

Miracky W. and Bortolotti B. (eds.) (2009), 'Weathering the Storm. Sovereign Wealth Funds In The Global Economic Crisis of 2008', Monitor-FEEM, SWF Annual Report 2008, April.

Miracky W., Barbary V., Fotak V. and Bortolotti B. (2009), 'Sovereign Wealth Fund Investment Behavior. Analysis of sovereign wealth fund transactions during Q3 2009', FEEM and Monitor Group, December.

Miracky W., Dyer D., Fisher D., Goldner T., Lagarde L. and Piedrahita V. (2008), 'Assessing the Risks. The Behaviours of Sovereign Wealth Funds In The Global Economy', Monitor Group, June.

Monk A. (2008), 'Recasting the Sovereign Wealth Fund Debate: Trust, Legitimacy, and Governance', in Social Science Research Network (SSRN).

Mubadala (2008), Annual Report, available at: www.mubadala.ae/media-files/2009/04/30/20090430_mubadala-annual-report-Final-web.pdf

Mubadala Development Company (2009), Six Month Financial Statement, available at: www.mubadala.ae/media-files/2009/09/07/20090907_09-Final.pdf

National Pensions Reserve Fund (2009), NTMA Results and Business Review, December, available at:
www.nprf.ie/Publications/2010/NTMAResultsAndBusinessReview2009.pdf

New Mexico State Investment Council (2009), Third Quarter 2009 Investment Performance Report, September 30, available at: www.sic.state.nm.us/about.htm

Norges Bank Investment Management (NBIM) (2009), Government Pension Fund, Quarterly Report Q3 2009, September, available at:
www.norges-bank.no/upload/77444/q3%2009%20report.pdf

Nugée J. (2009), 'Sovereign Wealth Funds' Coming of Age: Unrivaled Titans to Uncertain Mortals', in *Vision*, vol. IV, issue 1, State Street Corporation, Boston, pp.3-10.

Obstfeld M., Shambaugh J.C. and Taylor A.M. (2008), 'Financial Stability, the Trilemma, and International Reserves', NBER Working Papers 14217, National Bureau of Economic Research.

OECD (2008a), Declaration on Sovereign Wealth Funds and Recipient Country Policies, June.

OECD (2008b), OECD General Investment Policy Principles.

OECD (2008c), OECD Guidance on recipient country policies towards SWFs, October 11

OECD (2008d), OECD Guidelines For Recipient Country Investment Policies Relating To National Security.

OECD (2008e), Sovereign Wealth Funds and Recipient Country Policies, Investment Committee Report, April 4.

Prost O., Parmentier H. and Hugon C. (2009), 'Fonds Souverains: quelle réglementation Européenne?', in *Revue d'Economie Financière*, special issue 2009: *Sovereign Wealth Funds*, pp. 433-438.

Quadrio Curzio A. (1982), *The gold problem. Economic perspectives*, Oxford University Press, Oxford.

Quadrio Curzio A. (2008), 'Un Fondo sovrano con l'oro d'Europa' (A Sovereign Fund with Europe's Gold), in *Il Sole 24 Ore*, February 5.

Quadrio Curzio A. (2009), 'Per un Fondo di Euro-sviluppo' (For a Euro-Development Fund), in *Corriere della Sera*, February 28.

Quadrio Curzio A. and Miceli V. (2008), 'Fondi sovrani: i nuovi attori dell'economia mondiale' (Sovereign funds: new actors in the global economy), in *Il Mulino*, May/June, n. 3, pp. 555-566.

Quadrio Curzio A. and Miceli V. (2009), *I fondi sovrani*, Collana Farsi un'idea, Il Mulino, Bologna.

Rodrik D. (2006), 'The Social Cost of Foreign Exchange Reserves', NBER Working Paper, n. 11952, January.

Röller L.H. and Veron N. (2008), 'Safe and sound: an EU approach to sovereign investment', Bruegel Policy Brief, issue 08, November.

Rozanov A. (2005), 'Who holds the wealth of nations?', in *State Street Global Advisor*, August, pp. 1-4.

Setser B.W. (2008a), 'Sovereign Wealth Funds and Sovereign Power. The Strategic Consequences of American Indebtedness', Council on Foreign Relations, Special Report, n. 37.

Setser B.W. (2008b), 'Sovereign Wealth Funds: New Challenges from a Changing Landscape', Testimony before Subcommittee on Domestic and International Monetary Policy, Trade and Technology of the Financial Services Committee U.S. House of Representatives, September 10.

Setser B.W. and Ziemba R. (2009), 'Gcc Sovereign Funds – Reversal of Fortune', Working Paper, Council on Foreign Relations.

Subacchi P. (2009), 'SWFs and the Crisis: Putting a Brake on Growth', in Miracky W. and Bortolotti B. (eds.), 2009, *Weathering the Storm. Sovereign Wealth Funds In The Global Economic Crisis of 2008*, Monitor-FEEM, SWF Annual Report 2008, April, pp. 45-52.

Summers L. (2007), 'Funds that shake capitalist logic', in *Financial Times*, July 29.

Sun T. and Hesse H. (2009), 'Sovereign Wealth Funds and Financial Stability – An Event Study Analysis', IMF Working Paper 09/239.

Tovkailo M. and Pismennaya Y. (2010), 'VEB Gets Welfare Fund Cash for Infrastructure', in *Moscow Times*, January 13.

Truman E.M. (2007), 'Sovereign Wealth Funds: The Need for Greater Transparency and Accountability', Peterson Institute for International Economics Policy Brief, August.

Truman E.M. (2008a), 'A Blueprint for Sovereign Wealth Fund Best Practices', Peterson Institute for International Economics, Policy Brief Series n. PB08-3, Washington, D.C.

Truman E.M. (2008b), 'The Rise of Sovereign Wealth Funds: Impacts on US Foreign Policy and Economic Interests', Testimony before the Committee on Foreign Affairs, US House of Representatives, Washington, May 21.

US Department of Treasury (2007), Semiannual Report on International Economics and Exchange Rate Policies, Appendix III, June.

US Department of Treasury (2008), 'Treasury Reaches Agreement on Principles for Sovereign Wealth Fund Investment with Singapore and Abu Dhabi', hp-881, March 20.

Wyoming Treasurer's Office (2009), Wyoming State Investment Portfolio, at November 30, available at: treasurer.state.wy.us/pdf/portfoliostatus1109.pdf

Xiaohong O. and Peng L. (2009), 'CIC No Longer to Pay Interest to the State', in *Economic Observer*, August, 26.

Ziemba R. (2008), 'What Are Gcc Funds Buying? A Look at Their Investment Strategies', Rge Monitor Group.

Ziemba R. (2009), 'GCC Sovereigns: A Little Better Off', in RGE Monitor Group, May, available at:
www.roubini.com/globalmacro-monitor/257254/gcc_sovereigns_a_little_better_off

Websites

In addition the following websites contain detailed and updated information on SWFs:

www.futurefund.gov.au (Australia Future Fund)

www.ssf.gov.cn (China National Social Security Fund)

www.bcv.org.ve/fem/fem.asp (FEM)

www.minhda.cl/fondos_soberanos/fondo_de_reserva_info_valor.php (Chile's Ministry of Finance - Fondo de Reserva de Pensiones)

www.fondsdereserve.fr (Fonds des Reserves pour le Retraites)

www.ifswf.org/members-info.htm (International Forum of Sovereign Wealth Funds, IFSWF, Members information)

www.ipic.ae (International Petroleum Investment Company)

www.treasury.state.al.us/Content/07ATFpage.htm (Kay Ivey Alabama State Treasurer - Alabama Trust Fund)

www.kic.go.kr (Korea Investment Corporation)

www1.minfin.ru/en/nationalwealthfund (Ministry of Finance of the Russian Federation)

www1.minfin.ru/en/reservefund (Ministry of Finance of the Russian Federation)

www.mubadala.ae (Mubadala)

www.bmhc.bh/investor/ceo.asp (Mumtalakat institutional website – Ceo Annual Report 31st December 2007)

www.minfin.kz (Ministry of Finance of the Republic of Kazakhstan)

www.nzsuperfund.co.nz (New Zealand Superannuation Fund)

www.safe.gov.cn (SAFE)

www.oilfund.az (SOFAZ)

www.swfinstitute.org (Sovereign Wealth Fund Institute)

www.temasekholdings.com.sg (Temasek Holdings)

www.treas.gov/offices/international-affairs/cfius (United States Department of Treasury)

International Databases

EUROSTAT, Economy and Finance Database

IMF, Cofer Database

IMF, Data Template on International Reserves and Foreign Currency Liquidity

IMF, World Economic Outlook Database

UNCTAD, Foreign Direct Investment Database

WORLD BANK, Governance Matters 2009 – Worldwide Governance Indicators 1996-2008

Abbreviations and Acronyms

ADIA: Abu Dhabi Investment Authority

ADIC: Abu Dhabi Investment Council

ADNOC: Abu Dhabi National Oil Company

AGFF: Australian Government Future Fund

APRF: Alaska Permanent Fund

BIA: Brunei Investment Agency

CDC: Caisse des Dépôts et Consignations

CDP: Cassa Depositi e Prestiti

CIC: China Investment Corporation

CFIUS: Committee on Foreign Investment in the United States

CNOOC: China National Offshore Oil Corporation

DIC: Dubai Investment Corporation

ECB: European Central Bank

ECJ: European Court of Justice

EFTA: European Free Trade Association

EIA: Emirates Investment Authority

EIB: European Investment Bank

EMU: European Monetary Union

EP: European Parliament

ESF: European Sovereign Fund

ESSF: Economic and Social Stabilization Fund

EU: European Union

FEM: Macroeconomic Stabilization Fund

FINSA: Foreign Investment and National Security Act

GAPP: Generally Accepted Principles and Practices

GCC: Gulf Cooperation Countries

GIC: Government of Singapore Investment Corporation

GPF-G: Government Pension Fund – Global (Norway)

HKMA-IP: Hong Kong Monetary Authority – Investment Portfolio

ICD: Investment Corporation of Dubai

IFSWF: International Forum of Sovereign Wealth Funds

IMF: International Monetary Fund

IPIC: International Petroleum Investment Company

IRRC: Investor Responsibility Research Center Institute

IWG: International Working Group

KFW: Kreditanstalt für Wiederaufbau

KIA: Kuwait Investment Authority

KIC: Korean Investment Corporation

KNB: Khazanah Nasional Berhad

KNF: Kazakhstan National Fund

LAFICO: Libyan Arab Foreign Investment Company

LIA: Libyan Investment Authority

MOF: Ministry of Finance

NBIM: Norges Bank Investment Management

NPRF: National Pensions Reserve Fund

NSSF: National Social Security Fund (China)

NWF: National Wealth Fund (Russia)

OECD: Organization for Economic Cooperation and Development

PBoC: People Bank of China

P&O: Peninsula & Oriental Steam Navigation Company

PWMTF: Permanent Wyoming Mineral Trust Fund

QIA: Qatar Investment Authority

RAK: Ras Al-Khaima Investment Authority (UAE)

RF: Reserve Fund (Russia)

RSF: Russian Stabilization Fund (Russia)

SAFE: State Administration of Foreign Exchange (China)

SAMA: Saudi Arabian Monetary Agency

SCIC: State Capital Investment Corporation of Vietnam

SOE: State Owned Enterprise

SOFAZ: Azerbaijan State Oil Fund

SPRF: Sovereign Pension Reserve Fund

SSRF: Social Security Reserve Fund

SWF: Sovereign Wealth Fund

TEC: Treaty establishing the European Community

TFEU: Treaty on the Functioning of the European Union

UAE: United Arab Emirates

Other finance and professional titles from
Harriman House

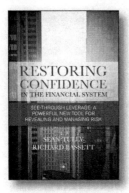

**Restoring Confidence In
The Financial System**
*See-through leverage: a
powerful new tool for revealing
and managing risk*
Sean Tully & Richard
Bassett
9781906659660

**Company valuation
under IFRS (2nd edition)**
*Interpreting and forecasting
accounts using
International Financial
Reporting Standards*
Nick Antill & Kenneth
Lee
9781905641772

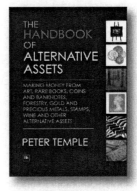

**The Handbook of
Alternative Assets**
*Making money from art, rare
books, coins and banknotes,
forestry, gold and precious
metals, stamps, wine and
other alternative assets*
Peter Temple
9781906659219

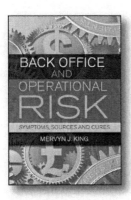

**Back Office and
Operational Risk**
*Symptoms, Sources and
Cures*
Mervyn J. King
9781906659363

**The Ultra High Net
Worth Banker's
Handbook**
Heinrich Weber &
Stephan Meier
9781905641758

Risk Pricing
*Using Quantum
Electrodynamics for
Higher Order Risks*
Dimitris N. Chorafas
9781906659370

Hh | Harriman House

Business titles from
Harriman House

The Maverick
*Dispatches from an
unrepentant capitalist*
Luke Johnson
9781905641406

**Selling Your Technology
Company for Maximum
Value**
*A comprehensive guide for
entrepreneurs*
Rupert Cook
9781905641925

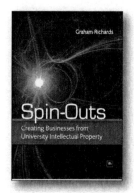

Spin-Outs
*Creating Businesses
from University
Intellectual Property*
Graham Richards
9781905641987

Eyewitness
*The Inside Story of a
Publishing Phenomenon*
Christopher Davis
9781906659196

In for a Penny
A Business Adventure
Peter Hargreaves
9781905641949

**Managing Through
Turbulent Times**
*The 7 rules of crisis
management*
Anthony Holmes
9781906659110

Hh   Harriman House

Economics titles from
Harriman House

The Myth of the Rational Market
A history of risk, reward and delusion on Wall Street
Justin Fox
9780060598990

The 21st-Century Case for a Managed Economy
The role of disequilibrium, feedback loops and scientific method in post-crash economics
Seán Harkin
9781906659547

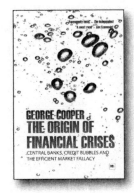

The Origin of Financial Crises
Central banks, credit bubbles and the efficient market fallacy
George Cooper
9781906659578

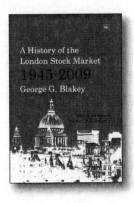

A History of the London Stock Market, 1945-2009
George C. Blakey
9781906659622

Petromania
Black gold, paper barrels and oil price bubbles
Daniel O'Sullivan
9781906659240

A Blueprint for Better Banking
Svenska Handelsbanken and a proven model for post-crash banking
Niels Kroner
9781906659318

Hh | Harriman House